Following The Spirit

Seeing Christian faith through
community eyes

First published by O Books, 2010
O Books is an imprint of John Hunt Publishing Ltd., The Bothy, Deershot Lodge, Park Lane, Ropley,
Hants, SO24 0BE, UK
office1@o-books.net
www.o-books.net

Distribution in:	South Africa
	Stephan Phillips (pty) Ltd
UK and Europe	Email: orders@stephanphillips.com
Orca Book Services Ltd	Tel: 27 21 4489839 Telefax: 27 21 4479879
tradeorders@orcabookservices.co.uk	
directorders@orcabookservices.co.uk	Text copyright Philip Bradshaw 2009
Tel: 01235 465521 Fax: 01235 465555	
Int. code (44)	Design: Stuart Davies
USA and Canada	ISBN: 978 1 84694 294 5
NBN	
custserv@nbnbooks.com	All rights reserved. Except for brief quotations
Tel: 1 800 462 6420 Fax: 1 800 338 4550	in critical articles or reviews, no part of this
	book may be reproduced in any manner without
Australia and New Zealand	prior written permission from the publishers.
Brumby Books	
sales@brumbybooks.com.au	The rights of Philip Bradshaw as author have
Tel: 61 3 9761 5535 Fax: 61 3 9761 7095	been asserted in accordance with the
	Copyright, Designs and Patents Act 1988.
Far East (offices in Singapore, Thailand,	
Hong Kong, Taiwan)	
Pansing Distribution Pte Ltd	
kemal@pansing.com	A CIP catalogue record for this book is available
Tel: 65 6319 9939 Fax: 65 6462 5761	from the British Library.

Printed by Digital Book Print

O Books operates a distinctive and ethical publishing philosophy in
all areas of its business, from its global network of authors to
production and worldwide distribution.

Following The Spirit

Seeing Christian faith through
community eyes

Philip Bradshaw SCC

BOOKS

Winchester, UK
Washington, USA

CONTENTS

III A THEOLOGICAL JOURNEY

IV EPILOGUE

To the congregation of St John's Redhill, who
listened patiently to many a sermon and
sometimes asked me for a copy.

Preface

Writing about living history is always tricky. Like political memoirs, there is no avoiding a personal take on events, especially if you happen to be a player yourself.

There is also a temptation, especially in religious writing, to produce a story of God's faithfulness that conveniently skates over the earthy human realities and struggles. Yet a mere recitation of facts can also be just as subjective, and will in any case omit most of the spiritual and theological subtext that is part of the real story.

I joined the Community of Celebration as a young man in the 1970s and it changed my life forever. That is one small element of the story, but even if the whole story is seen through those eyes it is no bad thing. People came to the Community from all sorts of backgrounds, but we all lived through the same events and talked the same talk. How I saw it may well reflect my particular perspective and religious background, but it will not be unrecognizable to others.

There is the story of what happened, which can be taken at whatever level you choose: a story of God's faithfulness over the years; a cautionary tale of mistakes and failures; an interesting account of a movement that influenced the church in a variety of ways.

Then there is the question of meaning. What was the point of it all? The issues that community life addressed were, and are, real ones for the church, especially at local level. On a range of issues, there was a characteristic "community" way of looking at

1

things that quite often stood in contrast to the way those same issues are typically related to in church life.

Finally there is the sense of spiritual and theological journey. It is impossible to live in a community for any length of time without being changed by it. In the church at large many people keep the same theological perspective for the whole of their lives. In the Community of Celebration, the very idea of "following the Spirit" implied movement, and for a conventional English churchgoer such as me it was perhaps the longest journey of all.

As I reflect now on a lifetime's journey, it seems to me that the central theme of the story is vocation and how it developed, principally for the Community but also for me personally. For that reason I have included some material on my own spiritual formation and calling to community life in Chapters 3 and 4. Occasionally I refer elsewhere to the way events impacted on my family.

My thanks go especially to Bill and Mimi Farra, who supplied much detail and corrected many factual points, and to all those former members who encouraged me to get on and write the story.

P.B.

Foreword

Eureka! Someone has dared to grasp the nettle: to tell the story of the Community of Celebration. From its genesis as an outreach ministry of an Episcopal church in Texas in the "hippie" sixties to its presence now as a small religious order centered in Aliquippa, Pennsylvania, there is much to explore.

Along the way there were exciting times of growth. There were world travels by the Fisherfolk who brought their engaging music with them to four continents. And there were times of testing. The sometimes alluring, sometimes troublesome history of the Community is described with grace and candor by the author, an Anglican priest who has himself been a member of the Community for 35 years.

He seems uniquely positioned to give readers two things, and does so. He takes us with him and his family on a personal, autobiographical journey which might be entitled, "...so you want to explore what it's like to live in community, eh?"

Needless to say, there are many laughs along the way, many hard adjustments too. But then, he does something else for us: turning his priestly gaze to the larger picture of what is happening in the church and in society, he helps us to a better understanding of the Community's relationship to both, and in so doing, of its *raison d'etre*.

The book accumulates theological weight as it progresses. It is as though the Community of Celebration's 40-year-long evolution has been poured into a funnel of corporate spirituality gleaned from life together, informed and enriched by an

3

Anglican discipline of worship.

Section II examines aspects of community life ranging from relationships to politics, allowing the reader to pursue topics of special interest. In the final chapter the author brings us back full-circle to the place he began in a depressed one-time steel town outside Pittsburgh. Here he poses the question, "So what difference has it all made?" Are there discernable effects when a small group of people plant themselves in a place like this for better or for worse, and provide a stable praying presence in a situation of obvious need? Or is the Community doing what one churchman called "pouring resources down a black hole"? Are the effects measurable? There are indications that they are; there are specific and encouraging signs.

The book leaves me challenged to reflect freshly on what it means to follow the Spirit in today's hurting world.

Betty Pulkingham

Chapter 1

Introduction: The Community Today

If you come into Aliquippa from the north, you join the line of traffic cruising lazily down Franklin Avenue, past St Titus' Roman Catholic Church on your left and then you enter a dogleg. To your right at this point you may notice a row of houses in two distinct blocks. The houses are clearly old, but the second block looks well kept, smartly painted with trim unfenced lawns bordering on a sidewalk that looks as if it has had a makeover in the not too distant past.

Ahead of you in the background is a bank of trees, vaguely reminding you (if you have the imagination) of the kind of landscape that must have greeted the early settlers in this part of the Ohio Valley two or three centuries ago. At this point Aliquippa seems not too bad a place, on the whole. But appearances are deceptive.

As you complete the dogleg, you come into the main street of Aliquippa. This is a street of store fronts in which almost every one is closed or boarded up. To the visitor it looks as if nothing much has happened here for years. There are very few people about.

If you were to turn off Franklin Avenue down Spring Street, you would immediately find yourself in a seedy unkempt area with a local reputation as the haunt of drug dealers.

This is not Los Angeles or Washington DC. But there are social problems aplenty in this town. Poverty, unemployment,

5

domestic violence, drugs. Murders are not all that common but they do happen on occasion. The blasting horns of emergency services or the wail of police sirens are commonplace, especially at night, but they hardly raise a ripple among the residents who have seen and heard it all before.

This is a town without much hope. But there are signs of hope for those who know the place and have eyes to see.

Down Franklin Avenue the Aliquippa Alliance struggles gamely to attract new business to the town and improve its profile. The Church Army is doing its bit, converting a derelict store into a café with space for local youth to hang out. Behind the scenes there are various projects and initiatives. Then there is the Community of Celebration. They occupy the smart section of the row houses. They have been based here since 1985, which was also the main turning point in the fortunes of the town.

Aliquippa belongs to the glory days of steel, which the regional center of Pittsburgh was internationally famous for. When market forces shifted the center of gravity elsewhere, factories began to close and Aliquippa was a one industry town. Almost overnight, its mixed population of African Americans, and a white community of largely Catholic Eastern European descent, were left without their only significant source of employment. To make matters worse, the company was unable to meet its pension obligations.

On its arrival, the Community of Celebration found itself plunged into the struggle to salvage something from the mess. Demonstrations against the closure of the factory and the pensions fiasco drew support from the solidarity of the recent influx of Community members who offered their skills in music leadership. The local Episcopal Church, practically next door to the Community of Celebration, voted with its feet to move to a more affluent neighborhood, leaving behind mainly the black, the elderly and the poor. The Community did its best to revive that too, providing the backbone of its worship life and holding its own daily prayers there.

Another big challenge was the property. The houses are built along the line of what the English call a terrace: basically in rows of identical houses. About a century old, they were nevertheless roomy with three floors and a basement. But they were badly in need of repair work, far more than a paint job. Remodeling and refurbishment were a major preoccupation in the early days of settlement at Aliquippa, drawing on the practical skills of members of the Community of Celebration as well as professional contractors.

One of the objectives of the Community was simply to become part of the fabric of the town. Members took various jobs, such as a teacher at the local school or a post at the Trinity Episcopal Seminary at Ambridge, the next town up the Ohio valley. One ordained member became chaplain to the local FBI, opening up a very different world of contacts. Another was invited to the board of the Aliquippa Alliance, linking the Community of Celebration to decisions and initiatives affecting the future of the town.

By reaching out to the town in this way, the Community came to understand its role as a ministry of presence. Smartening up the property was its most visible sign, letting people know that somebody cared about the place and was investing in it. Friendship lights in the upper windows during the Christmas season were a sign of hope, that something might yet rise phoenix-like from the ashes of the devastation of the 1980s. To the rear of the properties the yard area is common. To an English ear the word "yard" is strange, as it normally means an enclosed area with a ground of concrete or dirt and is used for a storage shed or for carrying out repair work. In America it can equally mean "garden," and in the Community of Celebration's case the whole of the common area at the back is a well kept stretch of grass where children can safely play, people can simply sit out in the open air, meals can be taken together and parties can be held there.

Today the Community of Celebration seems to live a more measured existence, as if the struggle and effort of the earlier years are over. This is due in part to some of the original members who settled in Aliquippa moving on. There are just six life vowed members left (with another two based in Britain). The Community is larger than the life vowed members and ebbs and flows as people with varying types of relationship to it come and go. The life vows reflect the maturity of the Community's development: the Episcopal Church of the United States gave it formal recognition as a religious community in 2001, one of its few non-monastic communities that are residential.

The maturity of the Community is also evident in the complex of buildings at one end of the row houses. Originally, a former undertaker's premises were taken over for use as offices. Integrated with this is now a purpose built chapel with sitting area, dining room and kitchen. On the other side of the office is another building, a large barn of a place that once belonged to the Salvation Army, now known as All Saints House. It is used for conferences and is still being developed for use in certain ministries.

Life in the Community of Celebration follows a settled pattern. The local Episcopal Church has long gone now, closed by the diocese of Pittsburgh when it became obvious that it was only the Community's presence that kept it going. In its place are the daily offices of morning, midday and evening prayer, together with weekly Eucharist, held in the Community's light and airy little chapel.

The inspiration for this pattern is the Benedictine model, albeit a modified version. Benedictine life is for the ordinary; it takes account of human frailties and limitations, and in this case that includes the family character of the Community with all its daily contingencies. In practice everyone normally attends the main daily offices and those who can attend at noon day.

The rhythm of life is punctuated with festivals and ministries of various sorts at certain points during the year. The Community sets great store on the cultivation of its relationships, and this often provides both the occasion and the resources for activities. An annual conference, for instance, draws together long standing supporters, who often include the speaker. Collaboration with the Church Army has involved provision of housing for Army staff and a jointly run training program on the premises for women from the local prison. During the summer contacts in churches elsewhere in the USA may bring a party of youth for a J2A (journey to adulthood) week. The young people have their own program and leaders but take part in the Community's worship.

A service which the Community of Celebration provides in the neighborhood is provision of housing at a reasonable rent. These are in great demand, for the houses are properly maintained and offer a safe place for children to grow up. But providing community housing is a costly and, at times, draining activity. The service is aimed at those who cannot afford decent housing and are likely to be turned down because of a poor credit rating. In addition to the demands of maintenance, this inevitably means working with tenants who fall behind with their rent, and only in the last resort, evicting them. Without that sanction, however, the scheme could not work.

Throughout the year there is a steady stream of visitors, many from overseas. Guests may come for a day or they may stay for months or even years. Some come for a personal retreat or to test their vocation, while others just want an experience of community or simply to visit friends. But they are also an important part of community life, participating in a variety of ways and connecting the Community of Celebration to a world beyond the immediate neighborhood.

Anyone visiting the Community will be struck by the important role that music plays in its life. The most ready forum

9

for this is its worship. Many a church or group that says the offices or has a mid-week Eucharist will dispense with music because musicians are not available and people are often uncomfortable singing in small numbers. Here singing is a regular feature of the offices and it is also clearly disciplined. Hymns and songs are not merely sung; they are sung well. The number of instruments that appear at larger services testifies to the presence of musicianship.

If they are not already aware of it, visitors will soon appreciate that music and worship are a special interest of the Community of Celebration and its wider network. A browse around the office will reveal many CDs and books with the "Celebration" logo and characteristic fish symbol. A closer look will show a wide variety of songs and many individuals credited who are not members of the Community today. It is clear that this Community has a history. There is a large picture on the wall, clearly made from a photograph, of a small cathedral on a Scottish island.

This is a Community with a past, which goes a long way further back than its arrival at Aliquippa. To appreciate its meaning, for those who know it and support it, we need to go back to its origins.

I THE EVOLUTION OF VOCATION

Chapter 2

Origin and beginnings in Britain

The story begins with Graham Pulkingham. It has to, because in so many ways he was the architect of the movement which affected many people's lives to an extraordinary degree and which ultimately became known as the Community of Celebration.

Graham was a priest in the Episcopal Church of the United States (ECUSA). As a young man he had married Betty Carr, an Instructor in Music Theory at the University of Texas, and together they had begun their family life in the pleasant city of Austin, where he was also based. In due course he received a call to an ailing church in Houston's inner city, with a charge from his bishop to either revive it or close it.

Graham was a strong man, a charismatic individual with a heart of compassion for the poor. But he met his match in the Church of the Redeemer. The congregation was small and growing old together, the last remnants of a once thriving community that had long since fled to the suburbs. Most of those who came to the church were commuters; they did not belong to that neighborhood any more.

They did not exactly welcome this man who came with a mission to Houston's poor. Nor, for that matter, did the neighborhood itself. Initial attempts to reach out to local people largely ended in failure, with the church being trashed to boot, earning the wrath of the conservative minded vestry.

Lesser individuals would have called a halt right there. Graham was made of sterner stuff, but even so it was a profoundly humbling experience. It was a crisis in his life, a point at which he found himself forced to search his own soul. As he himself later admitted, the problem was that he had grown to love the broken people that he ministered to, yet his own ministerial inadequacy had been brutally exposed.

But Graham was also a man who was open to God. You needed to be to go through an experience like that, and in Graham's case the depth of it was symbolized by the fact that it caused him to kneel in the middle of a New York street in an act of submission. He also received ministry from David Wilkerson, the Director of Teen Challenge in New York (an unlikely source, you might think, for a rather high church Episcopal Priest), leading to the experience known as baptism in the Holy Spirit.

All this happened in the mid 1960s, a period when the modern charismatic movement was just beginning to emerge in the mainline churches. Many were highly suspicious of it, but whatever the spiritual and psychological mechanisms were it was transformative. People had an inner sense of release that could break habits and transcend feelings of failure. They would speak in tongues and discover a new effectiveness to their own gifts, both spiritual and natural. Often they spoke of being washed or overwhelmed by love.

In this environment the expectation was that God would work actively in people's lives to heal diseases and restore broken souls. Stories of such healings abounded, together with many anecdotes of "signs and wonders" of the kind reported in the New Testament. It was with this kind of transformation of his life and ministry that Graham returned to the Redeemer (as his church was generally known).

Initially, it had little effect in the church itself. Beginning with the Pulkingham family, a little group began to meet together to worship. This was the seed of the community to come, but it grew outside the church, gradually drawing in others, some of whom were themselves lay ministers while others were the kind that Graham hoped to reach: people who were hurting or damaged.

At the core of this happening was a desire to spend time with each other, worshiping, sharing scriptures and sharing lives in an intensity of relationship that eventually had to find expression in physically being together in an intentional, committed way, sharing income, property and even homes. This became a model for the ministry of the church, a means whereby resources could be released and the unchurched could discover God without having to negotiate religious barriers.

Betty Pulkingham used her expertise in music to great effect. First, there were the needs of children to be considered. Later, there would be an outreach to the hippie culture of the day. There was also the challenge of congregational worship.

On each of these levels, it was important to develop worship in a way that was authentic for those involved. Yet even more important was the need to integrate such disparate groups into a single body.

This was the origin of the beautiful blended sound that later became the Community of Celebration's trademark. "Blending" was a feature not only of the sound itself but of the entire service of worship. Different kinds of songs and hymns were woven together into a unified tapestry of praise that became an expression of the body as a whole.

Liturgical worship, often regarded as stuffy or boring by those pursuing an ideal of freedom in worship, was thus transformed into a powerful medium for giving worshipers a sense of their spiritual identity.

Graham later identified four key elements in the formation of community at Redeemer, which came together in a very intense period in 1964-65.

The first stage was the gathering together of a community of sharing, which took as its "marching orders" passages from the

New Testament such as Acts 2, where the original Christians held everything in common, and Matthew 5, the Sermon on the Mount.

The inhabitants of the local neighborhood were the kind of people who would never enter the church, and Graham found that he identified with them more than he did with church members. Taking on the burden of the neighborhood had been highly stressful, threatening his marriage, but with this new ministry following baptism in the Holy Spirit healings began to take place and others came to be part of it. Soon a group was meeting together twice a day for a couple of hours or more at a time, reflecting on scriptures in the light of their situation. They began to share income and possessions, setting up a common bank account.

The second stage was the development of charismatic gifts. A number of these are listed in the New Testament and many people thought of them as the possession of certain individuals. But with this new group (eventually growing to 50-60 people) charismatic gifts were exercised as the ministry of the body. Often they seemed to merge into one another (a healing might happen in the context of a time of worship as opposed to a formal laying on of hands) and gifts might be manifested from different people rather than always from the same individuals. But because the group had learned to listen to one another and take what each person said seriously, amazing things happened.

By this time people had already learned to give up the right to make decisions over their own individual lives. The group was beginning to grow and was becoming cumbersome. The third stage saw the emergence of leaders, who were referred to as elders. These were naturally gifted people, trusted by the community because of their service to the group and to the ministry. They were elders because they were listened to, not because they were appointed. This cut across normal systems, for example ecclesiastical appointment, causing one or two who thought they should have been recognized as leaders to leave.

The fourth stage and perhaps most difficult of all was the opening up of family life. It began when a single person was taken into a family home who was neither "needy" nor any form of home help. The reason for doing it was to share resources, but it raised many issues to do with marriage and the relative importance of certain kinds of relationship. In coming to grips with this it was recognized that such an individual had to be accepted as a full adult family member. The home was not the family home; it was "our" home. This led to the understanding that the primary unit of society in the kingdom of God was the body of Christ (not the nuclear family), and the love relationship of brother to brother (or sister: gender was not the issue then as it would be today).

This confronted a great many cultural issues in western society.

Only after all this had been established did the community decide to support Graham in his role as priest at the Church of the Redeemer. The parish community there could not have existed without the intensive year creating a community outside the church. Graham believed that he had received a commission from God in the shape of a scripture from Ezekiel 2 and 3, which spoke of being sent "not to a people of foreign speech...but to the house of Israel."

He understood this to mean that his mission was to the church, who would find what he had to say pretty hard to take. What happened at the Church of the Redeemer was for the encouragement of the church worldwide. In time, that was also the mission of the new community in Britain and the ministry of the Fisherfolk.

The story of Redeemer has been told elsewhere[1]. As newlyweds in Britain, hungry for something dynamic and real in Christian experience, my wife and I heard about it and soaked

17

up all the information we could find. Within a few short years the Redeemer community would grow to several hundred strong, sharing homes and incomes in a more or less informal way. Its worship would attract international attention from across the English speaking world. By 1970 it would be receiving accolades from Guideposts Magazine and CBS Television.

One of those involved in the early days was Bill Farra, a young man who seemed destined for a legal career. His wife Shirley was ill, and in those heady times there was high expectation that she would be healed. But Shirley did not get better, and her death was a devastating blow to Bill. Graham was especially instrumental in helping him through the grief, and in the process despite the difference in their ages the two men became firm friends. Bill would later become one of the key ministers of the Community.

By temperament Graham was a foundation layer. By 1970 he was beginning to feel restless. He had already been at the church for nine years. Things were firmly established and he was beginning to look to the future. From his perspective there was just one problem with the Redeemer experience. It was the product of the charismatic movement, which was not widespread in the Anglican tradition even in America. There were some hotspots, such as Dennis Bennett's church in Seattle, but "Pentecostal" type experience tended to be concentrated in non-liturgical, non-Episcopal traditions.

Already there were signs of the kind of religion that that could lead to. There was the movement labeled as "heavy shepherding," a very authoritarian pastoral approach with a strong emphasis on deliverance from spirits. Later there would be popular movements such as the "prophets" emanating out of Kansas City. To Graham these kinds of things were the seeds of "charismania" and he did not want to be tarred with that kind of brush. If what had happened at Redeemer was to be authenticated by the Anglican Church as a whole, Graham reasoned that it had to be accepted by the mother church, the Church of

England. Only then would it stand a chance of being accepted by the English speaking churches of Australia, New Zealand and South Africa. As things stood, it was not only a "charismatic" oddity but it was also an American thing; and in the eyes of the rest of the world "American" meant wild and woolly.

So in 1971 Graham and Bill made a trip to England, speaking at a conference at Ashburnham. This raised a good deal of interest. At that time the main agency for promoting the charismatic movement, particularly in the Anglican Church, was the Fountain Trust, of which Michael Harper was the Director. In May 1972 he suggested Graham consider a serious trip, bringing with him his entire extended household. He arranged a number of clergy conferences, including one in the Coventry area.

One of Graham's household was Bill Farra, then in New Zealand with the traveling team from Redeemer. He joined Graham on a trip to Coventry, at which the recently made TV film about Redeemer, *Following the Spirit*, was shown. One of the clergy, Michael Hobbs, the Vicar of St. Philip's Potters Green, asked Graham if Bill could come and spend time in his parish as he had done in other places, and Cuthbert Bardsley, then Bishop of Coventry, gave his assent to the idea.

Never one to miss an opportunity, Graham replied in true community style that "if you take Bill you take me and all my household." Michael Hobbs gulped but agreed. It was a brave thing to do because it was one thing to take on a single young man in his 20s and quite another to take on a person like Graham Pulkingham and his entire support group. But Cuthbert Bardsley gave his support, and even helped to procure a property, a three bedroom house in a local housing estate. The garage was converted into a dining room and the dining room into a bedroom to make four bedrooms, but even so it was a tight squeeze for several adults and children.

Graham continued to travel in this period, so Bill Farra and another member of the Pulkingham household, Douglas

Kohnahrens, would meet with Michael Hobbs in the mornings while Betty Pulkingham worked with the worship life of the church. The little congregation (only six came on the first Sunday, plus the people from the Community) grew like Topsy, and soon English people wanted to be involved.

Clifford and Heather Booth had a larger house than the one the group from Houston were using. Catching the community spirit, they offered to swap houses. The Community was beginning to grow. By November 1972 it numbered 16, and within a few months it would increase to 27.

It was not long before all the human problems of living and working together at close quarters began to emerge. There were distinct cultural differences between the Americans and the British. In church, for example, the British did not necessarily see numbers as a measure of success; in fact, there was something slightly suspect about that, though it was hard to put a finger on it. It could have been down to English reserve, or it may have been due to an underlying fear of losing control to the Americans. At home, too, there were big cultural differences. Americans are very direct; they had a hard time with the indirect English way. It took a long time to learn that "would you like the salt?" really meant "would you please pass me the salt?" But there were also differences between the British themselves, based on deep rooted class distinctions. For some, tea was the main meal of the day, while for others children had tea and adults ate dinner or supper later on.

It all made for an interesting life. But this is the very stuff of community, working out differences and discovering what is really important whilst following a vision of life in Christ together.

The Fountain Trust created many openings for Graham that might not otherwise have been available, although it was also the case that the Community was the Trust's biggest calling card and in that sense the relationship was symbiotic up to a point. Thus in

1973 the Fountain Trust organized a major conference in Nottingham featuring Graham Pulkingham and the Fisherfolk (the Community's traveling team), which was attended by many international delegates.

The effect of the conference was to greatly increase interest and boost the numbers of people wanting to join the Community of Celebration from all over the English speaking world. It was obvious that another much larger property would have to be found. A mansion in the Coventry area came up for auction, and Graham and Bill attended. The Community of Celebration had a financial limit (which Bill already thought was beyond their capability) but it was not enough. Graham, not a man to be easily dissuaded by obstacles, wanted to go further, but Bill finally managed to convince him that it would be a disaster.

Graham was depressed by that episode but a little later Betty Pulkingham and Virginia Withey (another member of the Pulkingham household) happened to be in Slough when they bumped into Fr. Anthony, a monk they knew from St Gregory's Abbey in Michigan. After the initial surprise at having come from across the world to meet by chance in a street in Slough, conversation moved to the current preoccupation with the Community's need for property. Fr. Anthony told Betty and Virginia that the Benedictine monks at Nashdom Abbey near Slough had recently inherited a large property from the Sisters of the Good Shepherd. It was one of those incidents that always seemed to be happening in those days, as if God was opening doors and leading the way.

The Community had no previous connection with Nashdom Abbey but a meeting was arranged with the Abbot, Augustine Morris. Eventually it was agreed that the need of the Community met the monks' need to do something with the property, and so in late 1973 an advance party from Coventry of 12 people moved into Yeldall Manor. It was in a very run down state and barely habitable. Ruth Wieting and Tim Whipple, members of one of the

Fisherfolk teams, were appointed as coordinators of the clean up operation. Their efforts came not a moment too soon.

The acute problem of space at Coventry was illustrated by the fact that when Bill Farra and Mimi Armstrong married it presented an immediate headache in terms of bedrooms. People had to move around and some moved out to stay with neighbors, according to the traveling schedule and who happened to be at home.

Other issues needed to be addressed. For one thing, the community needed a name. For another, there needed to be some instrument for holding assets and allowing people to donate their support. The first was easily solved. "It will be called the Community of Celebration," Graham announced when the subject came up — rather to the surprise of some who thought such decisions were made corporately! But the reality was that the community was Graham's vision. The issue of assets and donated income was dealt with by setting up a registered charity, the Community of Celebration Christian Trust or CCCT for short.

Yeldall Manor is not far from Beaconsfield Baptist Church, where several individuals got involved as well as others in the local area. One of these was Dr. Desmond Orr, a director of the scientific instruments manufacturer Perkin Elmer and an elder at Beaconsfield. He became a trustee of CCCT and moved into Yeldall Manor with his family, as did several others from Beaconsfield and Gold Hill Baptist Churches. A vision began to develop of training church leaders in the ministry and the lifestyle.

Although there was no particular priority in allocating resources, in some ways this latest development, although low profile, was seen as more important than sending teams out. After the Nottingham conference, Fisherfolk ministry exploded. Festivals of praise in a series of cathedrals satisfied the Fountain Trust agenda whilst giving the Community a lot more exposure. Connections were made at big events with significant people such as Frank Lake, the Christian psychiatrist, or Bill Burnett, the Bishop of Grahamstown in South Africa (later Archbishop of Cape Town). Richard Holloway in the Church Times spoke of the Fisherfolk as a necessary ingredient in modern church worship. But at the same time the Community began to realize that the Fisherfolk were being used in many local church ministries simply as entertainment.

In addition to leading worship, on a ministry the teams would also teach. But this of necessity could only scratch the surface. Soon it became apparent that they were being asked to return to those churches and say the same thing over again. The goal of the Community (despite the impression many people formed) was actually not to get people to live in community. In that respect, talk of "a new way of living" was in some ways a distraction. The real vision was renewal of the worshiping life of the people of God. Incidental to that, the people from Houston had discovered that one of the most efficient ways of achieving it was to live in a different way, a way that released resources for doing ministry.

This linked naturally with the general charismatic agenda of empowering lay people through being filled with the Holy Spirit. There, as in the Community, there was an emphasis on developing gifts and ministries amongst ordinary people who were not academically or theologically trained. In the Community, the context for this was the Body of Christ with its many members inseparable from each other and interdependent. To further that vision it was considered vital for church leaders to experience the life and learn from it directly.

At this stage the Community was acting almost like a house church. Membership process was minimal or non-existent; that would not develop for seven or eight years. People were coming and going all the time until at its peak at the end of 1974 there were some 120 adults and children. Each week there was a service open to the public, which was packed. Visitors also frequently attended the Community's own Eucharist. It was in this kind of milieu that the Community showed how the empowering of lay people could develop.

Among the many that came to visit or to stay were a number of broken people. Some had quite serious problems: a young couple whose baby died while they were there; a young woman whose best friend was murdered on her 21st birthday; a man with a family who was in the process of undergoing a sex change operation.

These sad stories involved a host of emotional and psychological problems in varying degrees. Some were extreme, others simply problems of loneliness, rejection or poor self image. In the Community they found acceptance and healing, counsel and support. They were also a source of incidents, some of them quite bizarre, which produced a fund of Community stories. One very disturbed woman, for example, was in the habit of calling the police. One night, when the Community were having a "motor cycle" fancy dress party, there was a ring at the door. Mikel Kennedy answered it dressed like a Hell's Angel, only to be confronted by two police officers who wanted an explanation of what was going on.

All of this was the raw material for people who came to experience community life. If not exactly thrown in at the deep end, they had at least to learn how to swim. They would be assigned responsibilities or support roles that required them to learn how to deal with people and their problems — and how to deal with their own.

Thus the life drew out gifts that would never have been uncovered by formal training alone, even if there had been the resources to do it.

The only real structure to the Community at this stage was a system of elders and pastors. This was a hangover from earlier times at the Church of the Redeemer, later discarded. It did however introduce new blood into the Community leadership, including, importantly, from England. Men such as Desmond Orr and Michael Wood, both with long experience in business, brought a much needed expertise to activities such as record production, in addition to ministerial and pastoral experience. The community at Houston had produced four recordings, three of them from a coffee house ministry. People kept asking for copies of songs, and eventually it was easier to make a recording. It was not a serious commercial venture, because the United States market is vast and the community in Houston did not have the nationwide exposure that the Community of Celebration had in Britain. The fourth album, *God's People Give Thanks*, was a recording of congregational worship at the Church of the Redeemer. At that stage it was thought that as the church was not in the business of record production perhaps some other church publishing organization would take it on. An agreement was entered into with the Roman Catholic GIA Publications. Not only did they have production and marketing rights, but also, in exchange for $1,000 a record, they were assigned the copyrights.

In hindsight this was a major blunder, later compared by Bill Farra to Esau selling his birthright. The music was immensely popular, and the businessmen at Yeldall Manor saw how it could be a significant means of support for the Community. Accordingly, one of the steps taken at Yeldall was to set up a business framework for record production and ownership of copyrights. Little could be done about the past, but Betty Pulkingham did add new sections to the *King of Glory* Mass (the most widely used of all her settings) and to this day it is owned half and half by the Community and GIA.

Although there were many musicians and songwriters, Betty Pulkingham and Mimi Farra were central to this new thrust of making the music widely available. A contract was secured with the publishers Hodder and Stoughton for the production of a songbook, *Sound of Living Waters*, who asked that Betty Pulkingham and Jeanne Harper be the named editors although

Mimi Farra was also integral to the editing process and would be named as co-editor in later publications. It was an instant best seller, leading to production of the Community's first recording in Britain, *Songs from Sound of Living Waters*. A second songbook, *Fresh Sounds*, was commissioned and another record made of the same name. A third record, *Celebrate the Feast*, featured the full *King of Glory* Mass. It was recorded at Oxford, together with friends from Nashdom Abbey.

These early projects became the foundation of the Community of Celebration's business arm, generally known as Celebration Services. It involved many individuals in rehearsal and recording, music preparation, copyright administration and dealing with the public. In this period there were three Fisherfolk teams constantly traveling, requiring waves of new people to be brought over from the USA (although English talent was also trained as part of the teams). In addition to Yeldall, the Community had managed to buy another substantial property, known as The Thatched House, in the nearby village of Wargrave. Yet still it was not enough. At one stage, for instance, members of the Fisherfolk were sleeping in 3-tier bunks in dormitory accommodation. Once more the need for space was becoming acute.

---

[1] *A New Way of Living*, Michael Harper, Hodder and Stoughton, 1973

   Gathered for Power, Graham Pulkingham, Morehouse-Barlow Co., 1972
   (British edition: Hodder and Stoughton, 1973)

   They Left their Nets, Graham Pulkingham, Morehouse-Barlow Co., 1973
   (British edition: Hodder and Stoughton, 1974)

Chapter 3

A personal story (1): the roots of vocation

How do people get to join a community? For many it just happens it seems, almost as if by accident. They happen to be around when something is going on, or they come into contact with someone connected. Maybe they hear about it and write in, asking if they can come and try it. But there is a deeper issue than the mere act of joining. There is also the question of vocation.

Living in Britain, 5000 miles away from the action at Redeemer, we were aware of what was going on only through reading books. We had no inkling that we would eventually become part of its famous offshoot, which at that early stage was not widely known. As it turned out, joining the Community of Celebration was a long term life decision. It was not an experiment or something that just happened. Vocation has longer roots than that, and much of the Community's subsequent history is intertwined with my own life story. In order to tell the Community story, as I saw it, I need to tell a little of my own faith journey and how vocation developed.

I was born into a Low Church evangelical family in England, with all the religious and cultural accretions that such a background entails. We had strong links to the faith missions that had their heyday in the late nineteenth and early twentieth centuries. Growing up, the ideals of giving one's life to God and living by faith were a major part of spiritual formation, whatever the practical realities may have been. That was where the heart was, so to speak, even if I couldn't see how I could ever do that myself. It was not the most likely background from which to join a community coming from what many in our circles would have seen as a rather high Anglican stable.

The context was the charismatic movement of the 1960s, a period of profound social change. Those were the days of hippies, communes, flower power and the sexual revolution, not to mention Martin Luther King, civil rights and the student riots. It was a time for re-evaluating everything that had gone before, including, for many people, religion.

Living through it, however, it was perhaps not so much the start of a journey as a turning point in a story that had already begun many years before. At least, that is how it seemed to me. What went before is just as important to me in understanding how vocation was shaped and formed and what the move to community living was all about.

Actually, formative though my early Christian grounding was, it was not my most fundamental experience of God. That occurred at an age (three or four) before religion had seriously penetrated my consciousness. It was a feeling that came to me out of the blue one day as an irresistible pull within, almost like a summons, but to what I had no clear idea. It was like an invitation to come away and explore a magic land where anything could happen, and it would occur frequently without warning. As a child it was often confused with an urge to travel beyond the far horizon, or with excitement at the scent of a pine forest or the sound of a running stream, but as I grew up it acquired the character of a call from the eternal.

It never went away, and I was grateful for it later. In our spiritual tradition the way you came to faith was to invite Jesus into your heart, which I did at the age of seven thanks to my mother who used to have us kneel at the fireside to say our prayers before bedtime. It was a foundation on which much would be built, but by the time adolescence came along the accretion of religious baggage that went with it was almost too much to bear. The discrepancy between what seemed to be expected and what was achievable made a lot of religious input indigestible.

What did remain constant was the sense of call. It certainly made me curious about what really happened in Biblical times, and I also wanted to know if God was as predictable as some would have us believe; but I struggled to make sense of a relationship to God that was real and yet which seemed almost independent of religion and its requirements. At least the examples of young men and women who had given up their careers and even their lives for God were inspiring. I felt I didn't want my life to sink into the "middle class rut," a conventional career walking the treadmill of office life to pay off a mortgage.

These concerns faded into the background at Oxford, which was incredibly stimulating on all sorts of levels. At first it was simply mind expanding. The feeling was we were all young, in one of the most exciting places in the world, and the future was ours for good or ill. So far as Christianity was concerned, there were plenty of high powered speakers to hold the interest and respect of evangelical students. Nevertheless, after a couple of years I found myself becoming more and more restless.

It was fashionable amongst students to have doubts or even to adopt extremist views, but my struggle had less to do with intellectual problems than with the entire milieu of religion. The evangelical student unions had been founded in order to counteract the challenge of liberalism, with the result that the main focus of things in those days seemed to be on dotting the "Is" and crossing the "Ts" of theological purity. If that was the main point of being a Christian, I felt I could do without it, especially as (in my experience) it failed to deliver the goods.

Rather than being an enriching, fulfilling experience, theological debate seemed only to make religious life more

29

complicated, increasing the sense of guilt at not being able to keep to its exacting standards. Previously I had had a rather vague idea that Oxford would in some way be a gateway to the kind of Christian life that I wanted, but I came to realize that in spiritual terms I had got myself lost in a blind alley somehow.

That was an important milestone. One day, reaching deep within myself, I prayed a truly honest prayer. I told God I was willing to go anywhere and do anything, but he was going to have to do something himself from that point on. I had had enough of trying religious answers that didn't work. Unless God did something, religion in all its forms would be on the shelf until further notice.

Leaving Oxford, I began a career in heavy industry and the next couple of years were among the happiest of my life. What genuinely surprised me was that instead of losing my faith I got back in touch with the God I had known since childhood. I didn't go to church, quit reading the Bible and cared little for the many religious dictums that had previously governed my life and which now seemed petty. Yet God now seemed more real than ever, an intimate friend who had no judgment and wagged no fingers, someone I felt I could take with me anywhere, whatever I did. Those were heady days.

The experience of heavy industry (mining, in my case) led to a political awakening, again not so much intellectually as in a visceral sense. Working in the mines and living in mining communities, it was impossible not to absorb something of their outlook. There was a much stronger community spirit than I was used to. Life was viewed from the standpoint of those at the bottom of the heap. Issues of health, safety, welfare and poverty were the constant concern, together with the attendant desire for justice. These were not abstract issues; they were rooted in real lives and people's stories.

At that stage my religious life was on the back burner, but I knew it could never be quite the same again after that. If I ever returned to it, it would have to incorporate this new consciousness in some form or other.

One day a friend invited me to a meeting about the latest "Holy Spirit" movement that was creeping through the church. I was torn between aversion to all things religious and curiosity: curious because the charismatic movement claimed to make God real, which was the very thing that seemed lacking in the doctrinal religion of my background. So I went, and was quite surprised at the result.

I was open to any kind of experience if it worked, so I asked God to "do it" for me if it was real. What was referred to as "baptism in the Holy Spirit" was not overwhelming at first (at least, not in my case) but it did have genuine outcomes. First, there was a deep sense of peace, and rather weirdly I found myself completely unable to join in criticism of the speaker afterwards, despite the fact that he had talked a bit like Amos addressing the Israelites, and would have got up my nose too if I had taken him at all seriously. Later, a smoking habit was broken by the instantaneous disappearance of addiction to nicotine — an event so unexpected I could hardly believe it. A little later still, I tried speaking in tongues, which was supposed to be the main evidence of baptism in the Holy Spirit though it was very controversial. Since I had little patience with religious arguments, I just plunged in and it soon became a natural element in my experience — very useful for reigniting prayer life and also for when words failed or seemed superfluous.

After that I began to dip a toe back into church life, though with a very different outlook than before. Following marriage we decided to attend a church with lots of "charismatic" life and activity and for a time life was comfortable enough. But then I was disconcerted to find the old restlessness returning.

To a degree, it was the same problem as before. A movement that had begun as a direct encounter with God, transcending religious barriers, now seemed to be degenerating into just another movement with its own characteristic language and codes of practice. To fit in, you felt you had to say and do the right things. But more than that, when you really got down to it, I wondered how much difference any of it really made.

Certainly there was plenty of commitment on the part of some in our church, both financially and in terms of time and effort. A lot of good was done, in people's lives, as a result of many activities and initiatives. Yet aside from their enthusiasms, church people looked very little different from anyone else, on the whole. It was as if religion barely scratched the surface of life as everybody lived it. We had a neighbor, who was very active in the local community. I wondered if there was any objective difference between his way of life and ours.

When I received a call from God to join the Community of Celebration, it was very much in line with the expectations of charismatic experience at the time. But underneath it were a number of unresolved feelings about God and religion. Church often seemed as much a cultural phenomenon as anything, reflecting the values and mores of secular society to a large extent. It did lots of good, but I suppose at root I was *bored* with that kind of life. In retrospect, another way to look at the call to community could be to say that it was a moment in time when all the unresolved conflicts of years past suddenly clicked into place. These conflicts form a kind of backdrop for my description of the Community of Celebration in this book. They are my issues, to be sure, but they are not totally personal. They derive from the context in which the church found itself in those days, a context with which many Christians still struggle today.

Take, for example, the question of calling. It is not a job or a role, which one is directed to take up. In its deepest sense it is something you almost have to do in order to be true to yourself. Within the church many people feel this, which (like me) they may describe as a desire to give their lives to God. But there are very few opportunities to do it, and most of them don't fit the average person. Thus, although no doubt some Community members were there mainly for the experience, for others it was perhaps a matter of calling in this deeper sense (i.e. an opportunity to give their lives that was largely denied them in ordinary church life), and that is a significant part of the Community's meaning for them, as it was for me.

Another element is the desire, expressed by me in terms of wanting to avoid the middle class rut and by others in terms of not being just "Sunday" Christians, for a Christianity that cuts some ice, that does not just deal with individual problems and needs but also addresses the structures and powers that control everybody's lives and the unquestioned assumptions underlying them. Community life was a way of doing that. For me, it was also the answer to a lifelong inarticulate search for a way to make sense of the inspiring stories I had read as a boy, of people who lived by faith. Effectively, this was a contemporary way to do it.

Then there is the question of religion and the role that it plays in Christian faith. Members of the Community came from all sorts of church backgrounds, but one thing most of them had in common was that they were products of the charismatic movement. The role of the Holy Spirit was central to the Community's identity; it transcended religious differences and demonstrated that at the core of living Christianity is not theology but a spirit. That was extremely important to me in handling the pressure of conformist religion, but in general it was also true for most people. In church life, however, religious formation often seemed to take precedence over spiritual formation, though it was not always easy to distinguish between them. The difference was immediately apparent in Jesus' time, however, and community life had a strong emphasis on realizing the sayings of Jesus.

Thus there was more to the charismatic movement than the recovery of a lost experience; in many ways it opened up a new perspective on religion and its relationship to faith. The emphasis on spirit as opposed to law has implications for the church that have yet to be fully worked through even today. In the Community we felt we were exploring many of those implications in a real time, practical sort of way — as opposed to a heady theoretical approach, which expended most of its energy in debating the issues.

What the Community was most known for was its worship, which people experienced mainly through its music. But the music was just the tip of the iceberg.

Worship was about giving oneself to God, which in practical terms meant giving oneself to others in love and spiritual friendship. Out of that came ministry, which was not confined by the restrictions of ordinary living. It was a life that demanded everything, yet at the same time everybody — minister and ministered to alike — was fed.

After being part of it for a while, I realized that my old restlessness was gone. Whatever I had been searching for in the past, I was now home.

Chapter 4

A personal story (2): first taste of community

One sunny day in the 1970s, a red Volvo drove a little gingerly along a busy English road that would lead eventually to what looked like a Victorian manor house, hidden away in a secluded spot in rural Berkshire. The car was packed to the roof with personal possessions, including a dismantled wardrobe. The possessions were ours; the car belonged to someone else. This was the way you moved into community: not with a professional removal company but in a do-it-yourself exercise with various Community members pitching in.

We were a young family, with children of four and two, so we had more goods and chattels than most. We had to leave most of our stuff behind until we decided what to do with it, but even so we had more than we could easily manage. Yeldall Manor, the latest home of the Community of Celebration, was a former convent. The two rooms we were allocated were tiny, our double bed practically filling the former nun's cell which was to be our first taste of community life. But we accepted it cheerfully enough. For us it was an adventure, a major milestone, the first day of the rest of our lives.

Getting there had been quite a long journey. Having been born into Christian families, we had both grown up in an evangelical background and as young adults had embraced the charismatic movement because of its fresh approach that seemed to promise something new and real in Christian experience.

Our vocation to community life had begun in a suitably dramatic way, when I felt as if I had heard God speaking to me in an audible voice. I was in a meeting at the time, and the force of it was like an electric shock, almost knocking me off my chair. I reckoned I knew something of what Paul was talking about in his description of the Damascus Road, although no-one else seemed to notice.

How that led to the Community of Celebration was a process. The original context had nothing to do with community as such; it was more to do with a vision of pooling assets for the sake of the ministry. The Community had only just arrived in Britain at that time, and we were more familiar with its origins at the Church of the Redeemer in Houston, which we had read about in various books. The stories coming out of Houston offered one example of sharing resources. They were also interesting to me because the lifestyle made "living by faith" a possibility. They looked like a way to experience what faith in God meant in a modern, materialistic post-war world.

Part of the process involved taking into our home a former Hell's Angel, who had been almost killed in a head on crash with a bus. Christians in our circles were fond of talking about "loving one another," which always had a sentimental sound to me. The reality of it was hard, in fact impossible when we tried to incor-porate someone else into our small, middle class family. So here was another element. The command to love became a possibility when the pain of it was shared in community life. Christianity — the genuine article as opposed to cultural practice — seemed to make much more sense in a communal setting.

In 1973, when an advance party first went to Yeldall Manor, we heard about it and went to see Graham Pulkingham. He did his best to dissuade us from joining the Community, but the more he talked the more convinced we were that this was the right course for us. Months passed as we spent as much time as we could taking part in Community work crews and attending meetings. One day, we received an invitation: "Come and join us."

Now, here we were. It was with a slight feeling of trepidation that we made our way into the dining room for our first evening meal. At home, meals were always a bit of a battle with the kids, especially where vegetables were involved. In community in those days, we knew the ethos was that you ate everything on your plate. You could ask for a "no thank you" helping, but you ate it all, and that rule applied to the children too. On this occasion, chili con carne was on the menu.

It so happened that on this evening the local landowner, Lord Remnant, had been invited to supper. The last thing we wanted was a scene in the crowded dining room. When the meal arrived, to me the chili tasted like it was on fire. Afterwards I heard two versions of the story. One was that the cook that night, a Canadian, had mixed up North American and English table-spoon measures. The other was that a recipe for three table-spoons of chili powder had been read as *thirty*. Either way, the meal was a fiery concoction. Everyone struggled with the taste and with their embarrassment for Lord Remnant, but what amazed me was our little four year old who seemed to quite like it. It was his first taste of anything hot.

That incident was just one of many that were duly added to the folklore of community life. Life in community was a combination of the serious and the absurd. Laughter was an essential ingredient. Paradoxically, part of taking one another seriously was not taking things *too* seriously. It gave people room to breathe. It enabled them to feel accepted and respected for who they were, which many of them never felt in normal social life, including (and perhaps especially) in church.

In some respects life was much the same as in any normal family. Children had to be taken to school. There were the usual chores: cooking, cleaning, laundry, shopping, gardening, maintenance. Some individuals went to work every day in their secular jobs. What made it different were the economies of scale achieved by sharing resources and the general ethos of doing things corporately. Thus children would travel to school in a minibus, in most cases not driven by their parent. Rotas were the order of the day for many household tasks. Work crews took care of many jobs needing practical expertise.

Yeldall was a big place. Some people liked to call it a zoo. At its peak there were some 120 people living there, including about 35 children. To make it manageable it was split up into "households," which operated as separate units with their own finances. Each would start the day with "sharing," which involved offering one's own reflections on the scripture for the day, followed by a summary which was seen as God's word for the group. In the evening the whole Community would come together for "chapel," which was a time of informal worship with a lot of singing.

There were so many comings and goings in those days that the Community was inherently unstable. Some came for training; some for healing; some (including many from Houston) to resource the ministry; some (from all over the English speaking world) just to experience community. Others were leaving, perhaps moving on in their lives or joining with others to establish a community elsewhere. We had hardly had time to settle in before we were introduced to a regular feature of community life: household moves.

Changes were often precipitated by people joining or leaving, but there were also special considerations such as the needs of children or the requirement that an individual might have for support in their life. Sometimes a household would be based around a ministry, such as an outreach team or a pastoral ministry. All households were seen as pastoral units and great care was taken over choosing their make-up. A general move was referred to as a "fruit basket turnover."

When it came to moving day it was a case of take up your bed and walk. Usually there would be people on hand to help, but it was another reason for traveling light as far as possible. Over the years, there would be many lost items last seen at some point before a household move. On our first occasion, we moved into a small household together with one of the leaders from Houston, Jerry Barker, and a single parent family consisting of mother and son.

The purpose of this household was twofold: to provide support for the single mother, who clearly had some troubling issues in her life, and to give us a bit of training in how to deal with such situations. In these circumstances we learned an enormous amount in a very short time, as did many others who joined the Community of Celebration.

In those days the charismatic origins of the Community were still very much in evidence, and it was fascinating to see the overlap between normal human discernment and the gifts of the Spirit. Our single parent housemate insisted she wanted to be part of the Community, yet there was something about her insistence that did not add up. One day Jerry seemed a bit exercised about something and then finally said, "I think you want to get married." He had hit the nail on the head. That was the real agenda — she was looking for a husband. We were able to talk about it and not long afterwards she left.

That household experience lasted just ten weeks before it was time to move again. That was the way it was in those days: an extremely dynamic life.

Community jargon included phrases such as "constant change is here to stay." Change was equated with "following the Spirit," meaning a willingness to do anything or go anywhere as the need arose, almost at the drop of a hat.

When Jerry Barker finally left Yeldall, along with a number of others, the Community held a party at which various awards were handed out. Jerry was given the "Pillar of Fire" award for the person who had made the most household moves.

Initially I continued my job in London, commuting daily while the family remained in the Community. I had always hated the daily rat race, and community life merely made me all the more eager to get out of it. Yet even here community had its moments.

At one time Graham had been giving some pastoral teaching on the subject of "the elder-younger relationship" (of which more later). Next day I was on the train in a packed carriage of the old type, a single compartment with two rows of seats facing each other. My normal habit was to submerge into a newspaper until the end of the journey, but on this occasion my companion was a young man who had a bit of a reputation for being an extrovert character. To my horror he suddenly produced an enormous bible and invited me to join him in a "sharing" session. Eight other English suits in the compartment looked as if their ears were flapping. I made some reply about having already done that, at which point with a disarming grin he announced to the whole compartment that he thought he would study more about the elder-younger relationship. I was never more thankful for a newspaper.

But it was in the context of ordinary daily life that you learned what it really meant to live in community. Individuals varied in the amount of personal space they felt they needed in order to make life tolerable. Some could hardly stand community life at all, but they were probably in the minority. What most people experienced were the normal irritations that arise when people are living and working together at close quarters. Because there was no "back door" to get away from the situation, these were magnified until personal traits and quirks became "issues." Habits and mannerisms, language and tone of voice, even the way a person dressed could eventually drive another person to fury.

Needless to say, such a pressure cooker could not exist without a controlled way of letting off steam. People were encouraged to talk about what bothered them rather than bottling it up until it came out in an explosion. Consequently a lot of time was spent in working out relationships, but this was not seen as a waste of time. On the contrary, it was life changing.

Over time, a hundred small reconciliations and acts of forgiveness led to a quality of relationship that is hard to describe in words. In general, it was not that the other person changed: *you* were the one who changed. It was like a gradual awakening to see the other person as they really were, and in so doing you learned the true meaning of love. Love was not passion, nor was it selfless altruism. The other did not become one's special friend, though many people did form deep friendships. To love was to embrace the other's humanity, warts and all, to affirm their dignity and to stay open to them. What happened in specific cases was the material that helped you learn the ethos of the Community as a whole.

It could be quite disconcerting, sometimes, to find oneself on the receiving end of this kind of acceptance. I recall one occasion when annoyance had built up in me to the point where I vented my feelings, albeit in a very rational sounding way. My expectation was that others present would be defensive or corrective or would just ignore me. Rather to my surprise I found people making friendly eye contact, listening to what I said and apparently taking it seriously, and offering their own perspective without emotional loading and with no sense of patronizing. Not only did it diffuse my feelings but it was far more effective in enabling me to confront what was going on within than a frontal attack.

For many people the very circumstances of corporate life brought up feelings. It was beyond their control, even though they knew that feelings were not the same thing as reality and to dump them on other people was inappropriate. It was recognized that such feelings were often a projection from a painful experience in the past. Consequently it was necessary for the

Community to make available pastoral facilitators who would either act as a broker to help the process of working out relationships or else provide a listening ear for individuals struggling with their own responses. In a few cases it seemed as if some individuals were almost dependent on their pastor.

More controversial, perhaps, was the practice of pastoral intervention. With so many people of diverse backgrounds and ages, trying to live a life of commitment to Christ that had already been established to a large extent at Houston, it was inevitable that behavior would be challenged. It was not simply a matter of personal relationships. The way some people related affected the whole community or at least their household. In some cases it called into question their suitability for community life at all. Some who had come from Houston referred to visits by certain elders as "meat axe sessions." At Yeldall, difficult personal issues would be dealt with by experienced individuals, but there was no doubt that they could, at times, be pretty confrontational.

In general, the gold standard was love. On one occasion, a community leader went into a bathroom and scooped up a handful of matted hair and muck from the drain hole. Going into a meeting, he threw the mess on to the floor in the midst of the assembled company with the words "That's how much we love one another!" The standard of love made for a pretty disciplined life, which was necessary not only to create an ethos amongst such a disparate group of people but also to establish the charism of the Community of Celebration: its corporate life in which we were all "members one of another."

The life itself, rather than the opinions or prejudices of individuals, was the force that pushed people beyond their barriers and their withdrawal mechanisms.

Not all issues could be resolved at the Yeldall community, which existed for a relatively short time. In regard to children, for example, mid-twentieth century American practice included smacking of small children, whereas Swedish attitudes in relation to authority in general (including children) were to respect the autonomy and boundaries of each individual. The English came somewhere in between. These cultural differences caused a certain amount of tension at times, but it seemed to me they should not be overstated.

The effect of the environment on those who were there for healing was remarkable.

A number of individuals troubled by a low self image or deep seated issues of anger soon blossomed into functioning members. The Community also had a specialized ministry of healing at that time. It was costly in terms of the resources required, but that was the whole point of living in community. One young woman had psychiatric problems that were quite severe. She would have had to be hospitalized, but the consultant psychiatrist at the Royal Berkshire Hospital agreed to let her remain in the Community's care. He recognized that the Community had more to offer her than the hospital ever could.

One of her symptoms was destructive and hysterical behavior. Clothes would be cut up and there was concern about how she might affect other members, especially the children. At one point it was necessary to lock her in an empty room of a nearby community house. She managed to get a window open and shouted to some passers by that she was being held a prisoner, which resulted in the police being called. On another occasion she attacked the man who was primarily responsible for supervising her care. He fell on the floor and pretended to be dead, which was a way of challenging the behavior and appealing to the adult. It had the desired effect. Eventually with stable daily support from a number of people, she recovered from her illness and was able to resume a normal life.

This kind of ministry was extremely costly both in terms of the numbers involved and the degree of commitment necessary. But it was not considered unusual. The spirit of the Community was that you did whatever was necessary. You could expect to have at least a room, though even that was not guaranteed. Single people in a ministry team had dormitory accommodation with bunk beds, while an older couple found themselves at one stage sleeping in a kind of landing area overlooking the entrance hall.

For us, the sacrifices of community life were mainly felt in relation to our children. Life in community is common life. Children were in no doubt who their parents were, but many of the things that traditionally happen within the nuclear family were shared. This meant you had to trust the concern of other adults for your children. Occasionally this might stretch you. I once had to rescue our two year old from a bath which was too hot. She was not burnt but looked a bit like a boiled beetroot. At another time the pressures on accommodation meant that we adults were sleeping in an old caravan which leaked, soaking our mattress, while the children were separated from us in the main house.

These were things you settled within yourself as part of the cost of your chosen vocation. But if the story gives the impression that children were neglected, that would be totally false. Children were in fact at the very heart of the Community's life, and an enormous amount of time and energy went into caring for their needs. "Children's ministry" was a name given to what was almost a community department. I was once part of it myself, during days off from my secular job. It was a fascinating experience for someone more used to a London office.

One child care program that ran for a while was known as the "Yeldall Yellers." This took care of younger children, releasing mothers for activities elsewhere. The children might be taken by minibus to some local attraction or other. But the most visible sign of children's inclusion was in worship and celebrations. Evening "chapel" featured simple songs, many of them written by Community members. At the weekly Eucharist, it was taken for granted that children of whatever age, from zero up, took part in the bread and wine. One of the Community members, Maggie

Durran, later wrote a book called *All Age Worship*[1], at a time when the concept was hardly known in the church at large.

Every week there was a celebration of some sort, a kind of party at which Community members would do a sketch or a funny turn. Occasionally a celebration would expand into a major event. There were a couple of carnivals, which involved everyone dressing up and in some cases creating the most amazing costumes. Or there might be a sports day, which was easy to do at Yeldall because of the large grounds.

As far as the outside world was concerned, what the Community was most well known for was its worship. Ministry teams of young people known as The Fisherfolk were constantly traveling. A high proportion of them were accomplished musicians, and they also made full use of other media such as drama, dance, poetry and so on. This attracted large numbers of people to visit the Community and caught the attention of radio and TV. I still recall the annoyance I felt on one occasion in the middle of a Eucharist. We were lining up to receive communion when I was elbowed unceremoniously out of the way by a TV cameraman desperate to get a shot of one of the children receiving.

To accommodate the interest, the Community held weekly evening meetings for the general public. Although these might include an address from someone such as Graham Pulkingham, the main attraction was the worship, or more accurately the sound of music in worship. It was quite unlike anything in any church at the time, a beautiful blended sound designed to reflect the spiritual reality of lives lived in unity with each other. It seemed as if people could hardly get enough of it. Within the Community it was part of daily life, evident not only in services but on many other occasions. Even if you felt you couldn't sing a note, you were expected to attend choir practice at which you learned how to do it and to overcome your inhibitions at opening your mouth.

Community members were prolific songwriters. At Yeldall, new songs were emerging all the time. Many of them were very simple folk songs which could be sung as a round. But the sound spoke as powerfully as the words, because it provided a non-verbal experience that everyone recognized as a reflection of what they encountered in community life. At certain times even words became unnecessary. A common feature of charismatic worship is singing in the Spirit (not unlike speaking in tongues) where people sing without normal language and blend their voices. It can have a remarkably powerful effect.

For example, in one public meeting, a time was provided when anyone present could offer a prayer. One young man started praying loudly. The prayer went on and on and became a rant. It was hard to see how it would be stopped. Then I became aware that one of the Fisherfolk, Max Dyer, had started to play very quietly on his cello. Soon others began singing quietly, blending with the instrument. Still we could hear the ranting of the prayer. The sound swelled, until it drew in the whole room and reached a crescendo, by which time the young man's voice had been drowned. Then suddenly it died away and in the silence that followed you could have heard a pin drop. Such drama made our worship anything but routine, and it spoke to people on many different levels.

Demand for the Fisherfolk was such that the Community was forced to make a recording. The new record, called *Songs from Sound of Living Waters*, was circulated at first by mail order and at meetings. Then the office received a rather disgruntled phone call from a bookshop, saying he had been looking everywhere to find out who produced this record that people kept asking for, and was this the place? So began the commercial activity of the Community. We could not know it then, but it would affect many of our lives for years to come, and in some respects still does today.

Among many significant visitors to the Community were two bishops in the Diocese. One was the suffragan Bishop of

Buckingham, who visited on a Saturday night when the kids and the Fisherfolk were doing a "Winnie the Pooh" presentation. He told us that A.A. Milne had been a parishioner of his, and that he had known Christopher Robin as a little boy! The coincidence was a bit overwhelming for his young audience.

The other was the diocesan, Kenneth Woollcombe, Bishop of Oxford, who had formal jurisdiction as we were an Anglican community in his diocese. From the amount of spit and polish that we all had to put in beforehand, you would have thought we were being visited by royalty. But it was an important occasion, because for many of us it was the first time we had ever had to think about what we were or what church we belonged to. The Community was a melting pot of nationalities and churches from Roman Catholics to Evangelical Baptists. Now, when the bishop was asked what he thought of us, he said he saw us as a new form of religious order.

We had very little understanding of what that meant. But we understood that what we had joined was developmental and radically different from the church life we had left behind. Consequently when it came time for the Community of Celebration to vacate Yeldall Manor, we determined that we would not go back to our old life. The Community split into several groups, which were intending to start communities in various parts of the country. The structure of authority and leadership was such that you could not simply decide where you would go — you had to be invited — but there was room for negotiation. Until the way ahead became clearer, we negotiated to stay with a locally based group.

We felt we had lived a lifetime in a couple of years, but this was just the beginning of our community journey. Hundreds of others have lived in one or other of the Celebration communities, and each has their own unique story to tell. In those early years it was a very full life which affected people in different ways, yet in one sense in the same way: the taste of the Community's unique grace or charism in relationships would remain with most people forever, keeping them connected for decades.

1   Angel Press, 1987

Chapter 5

Life on a Scottish island

Space was not the only pressing issue facing the Community in 1975. Graham was still officially the Rector of the Church of the Redeemer and at this stage the Community was effectively an outreach of that church. He was able to import a large number of people from there, both to resource the increasing demands for ministry and to provide the milieu for new people to join and experience community life. One of the things that might seem odd when viewed with hindsight was that nothing was ever written down at Yeldall. People who joined were not told the precise terms on which they belonged, nor did they sign any form of contract. It was all by personal invitation.

The resulting vagueness meant that the source of authority ultimately went back to Graham himself. The leading figures, elders and pastors, were his trusted associates from Houston plus certain English church leaders who were there for training. Pastoral authority also flowed from this source. The elders met regularly to discuss community issues, but only rarely did anyone hear about the discussions, usually only when a major decision had been taken, when it would be carefully explained at a Community meeting.

But at the time few people questioned the system. If it seemed undemocratic, it also allowed for a lot of flexibility. In terms of finances, for example, it was up to individuals to determine how much they contributed to the common pot. The Community at this time was substantially supported from donations. On the whole, people simply trusted the decisions that were made, especially as negotiation was always possible. However influential he was, decisions were not seen as "Graham's" decisions because the ethos was corporate life — decisions came out of the sharing of hearts and minds committed to one another in love. It was actually Desmond Orr, an English leader, who was the titular head of the Community.

The first significant sign of a crack in this carefully nurtured ethos was an event that took place in the USA, the significance of which the English members hardly understood. The Church of the Redeemer's formal connection with the Community effectively came to an end in 1975. The way it happened was somewhat painful to Graham, even if necessary.

After he had moved to England, another priest at the church, Jeff Schiffmeyer, took over. As before, governance of the church was shared with a group of lay elders. Jeff was a gentle person, well suited to ministry in the environment of love that characterized Redeemer in Graham's time, but less comfortable with the power politics of a complex parish. Several of the strong supportive lay leaders had also gone to England, and in their place a new body of opinion formed which was attracted by the kind of ministry coming out of Fort Lauderdale in Florida, associated with men such as Derek Prince and Bob Mumford. For a while the whole pastoral ministry of the parish was being turned into a preoccupation with deliverance from demonic forces. The weight of this opinion, which "corporate decision making" required Jeff to support even though it meant risking his relationship with Graham, led to something of a crisis.

Graham still had enough authority to say that changes had to happen, but he was not about to reinvent himself in the parish. He was still officially the Rector, even though financial support from Redeemer had ended during the time in Coventry. The situation at Redeemer, coupled with other developments in Britain, now led to the termination of Graham's tenure as Rector.

In reality the question of Graham's position had to be addressed one way or the other, and he probably should have resigned earlier. But it was a big shift, emotionally, for those involved, though personal relationships with Redeemer continued and remained strong for decades.

Meanwhile the pressures of constantly living in the public eye, with the consequent demands for ministry and resources, were taking their toll in Britain. Yeldall Manor, which was in the south of England within easy commuting distance of London, was almost too accessible. Space continued to be at a premium. Something had to give.

Enquiries were made about the possibility of buying Yeldall, but the cost of bringing it up to scratch would be enormous. Michael Wood advised that it would be a bad investment. Then, one day, Graham and Bill were on a visit to St. Paul's Edinburgh, the Rector of which was Richard Holloway who had once written about the Fisherfolk in the Church Times. Someone who had just visited the island of Cumbrae in the Firth of Clyde said that the Cathedral of the Isles there was looking for an Episcopal group to move into the place. At present it was being occupied by Youth With A Mission, an independent group, which was contrary to its deed of trust.

On their way back south Graham and Bill took a detour via Cumbrae to take a look. It seemed a remote and Spartan kind of place, and they came back without forming any conclusions, but news clearly traveled fast for the very next day there was a phone call from the Bishop of Argyll and the Isles, Richard Wimbush. That began the process of taking out a 10 year lease on the property, regularizing Graham's position in Britain and enabling him to resign from Redeemer. Graham would be officially appointed Provost of the Cathedral, and to enable him to travel other priests in the Community would be licensed to supply a regular ministry.

The deal was done, and by mid 1975 the process was already under way of laboriously moving north. Everything at Yeldall was done on a shoestring, and true to form a clapped out old coach was used to transport a mini mountain of furniture and belongings. Most of the seats were stripped out and we all helped to pack it to the ceiling with goods, chattels, plants and animals before sending it on its way. It made several journeys on a wing and a prayer before reaching its final resting place at Cumbrae, where it was again pressed into service as a temporary office.

This was not the end of the Yeldall Community, however. That would not happen for another year or more. Only about half the Community went to Scotland, mainly (though not exclusively) Americans and those involved in music development. The other half remained until their future became clear.

It was about this time that a relationship began to develop with the Post Green Community. Post Green was the home of Sir Tom and Faith Lees, landowners in the south of England near Poole in Dorset. For a number of years they had been making their home and facilities available for Christian ministry, running annual camps and attracting various ministries such as a Bible School and a Sacred Dance Group. Post Green was also a center for counseling and healing ministry. It was a different kind of community than the Community of Celebration, but it involved a large number of gifted people.

Some time previously Tom and Faith, together with one of the community members, Jeanne Hinton, had visited Redeemer. They had been inspired by what they saw, and recognized that worship was an ingredient that was lacking or undeveloped in their own community life. Graham, too, had visited Post Green. Now, the possibility was raised of joining forces. It seemed a typical scenario, very common in community life, where two needs met. Post Green was in a position to house large numbers of people in a variety of properties, while the Community of Celebration could provide expertise in worship and household living, plus the nucleus of a traveling Fisherfolk team.

There were other reasons for the link up with Post Green, apart from the purely pragmatic. Post Green was a kindred spirit. It had a valid ministry and ethos of its own — the concept of a "city of refuge" that provided a place of safety for the wounded. There were advantages in joining with a body that was already established in England and that could provide some perspective on what was happening in the church in the 1970s. Not everyone was convinced that the arrangement would work, however. Some of the Post Green ministers left when Celebration arrived with its strong corporate ethos and Anglican commitment. Some Celebration members felt the two foundations were incompatible. But the arrangement was amicable enough, and integration did not initially provoke the kind of problems that arose later on. It looked a promising development.

Accordingly, in stages, people began to move from Yeldall to Post Green. We too were invited to go there. When moving day arrived, the van we had acquired for the job was packed by a Community member who prided himself on utilizing every cubic foot of space. It made it so heavy we were unable to travel at more than about 40 mph and we worried at every corner that it might turn over. But like our original journey to Yeldall, it was the start of a new chapter for us, with the ultimate destination unknown.

The contingent who had gone to Scotland a year earlier consisted of some 50-60 people. It was not an easy assignment. The harshness of life on Cumbrae has been described in Maggie Durran's book *The Wind at the Door*[1]. Ask anyone who lived there what it was like and the response is likely to be "Cold. Drafty." In modern terms, particularly for Americans who were used to conveniences and things that worked, it was primitive. At afternoon chapel heating was with gas fires fed from butane bottles. Those who sat too close were burned while those who sat further away shivered. Jackie Kemp, one of the first group to arrive, summed up the feeling: "They've sent us here to die!"

Why go to such a remote spot? Apart from the immediate pressing need to resolve the space crisis, there was a growing appreciation at Yeldall that intensive ministry was not producing the expected results. It took enormous resources but significant outcomes in the corporate life of the church were hard to discern. It was not a problem confined to the Church of England but had to do with the nature of church itself. It was possible to renew or reform the outward forms of worship, but the underlying spiritual changes that gave the Community's worship its power required an intentional approach that conflicted with the way most institutional churches operate. The feeling emerged that maybe it was time to draw back a bit from this dramatic life.

One of the main reasons for withdrawal from the spotlight was the need for space to carry on research and development. The continuous production of music to satisfy the public's insatiable demand required an enormous amount of work, researching resources, dealing with copyrights, preparing manuscripts, rehearsing. The production of songbooks was a major project in itself, let alone commercial recordings. Pastoral issues had arisen as a result of so many people coming together in such a short time, living such a demanding life. The way forward seemed to be to establish a stable base for international Fisherfolk ministry, with less frenetic traveling and more emphasis on training and conference ministry. Theologians such as Paul Felton would be part of this, providing the intellectual underpinning for the Community's life.

It needed somewhere a bit more removed from the mainstream. Cumbrae was certainly that, although in its own way it needed almost as much pioneer work on the premises as

Yeldall did. The Cathedral grounds were overgrown and the College of the Holy Spirit attached to it (actually two college buildings, north and south) needed work to adapt it to the needs of a sudden influx of a large group with furniture, office equipment and musical instruments. It was hard but most of the Community were young and up for it. In that first year a Fisherfolk training program was established, attracting people from England and as far away as Australia.

The Community had now been in Britain some three or four years, and by this time longer term personal issues were beginning to bubble to the surface. There was a felt need to put down roots so as to establish some sense of corporate identity. It had been impossible to do that in a situation like Houston, where there were so many needs, or at Yeldall, where traveling schedules meant there was hardly time to draw breath. Part of the problem had to do with lay ministry, particularly in the Anglican Church. Most Community members had no intention of becoming ordained, but if they weren't then who were they? In the eyes of the church they were just enthusiastic lay people with no responsibility for the church's ministry and the church had no particular responsibility for them.

The question lay members had to face was, if they were not going to take the ordination route, what were they doing with their lives? As far as they knew, what they were doing was not some passing fancy — it was what they intended to do with the rest of their lives — but what did it amount to? Were they just laity attached to some priest, and if so what happened when the priest disappeared? At this stage vocation did not have a clear shape. Now they were detached from their original parish church base there was a need for understanding of who they were and what their worship and common life was about. They needed some way to become recognized.

After about a year at Cumbrae an event took place which, though devastating at the time, actually focused this issue much more clearly. The north college building was destroyed in a fire. It happened on a cold February afternoon when the wind was blowing a gale and most of the Community were in a meeting. Bill Farra was in bed with the flu and a small child was asleep. He was woken by the smoke and the sound of the baby crying and rushed to get him out. The alarm was quickly raised and some belongings were salvaged but the building could not be saved. The local fire engine was inadequate and the Community could only watch helplessly as many of their possessions were destroyed.

Those displaced had nowhere to sleep. Local people rallied round and offered emergency accommodation. It was a major disorientation and to this day some have no idea who it was they stayed with. But it also helped build bridges with the islanders, with whom relations had not been altogether cordial up to that point.

From the islanders' point of view, the Community were a foreign import into their way of life. They had had previous experience of a hippie group and then YWAM, which was an American organization with an "in your face" style of evangelism promoting the "four spiritual laws." Now here was yet another weird American commune, as they saw it, taking over "their" cathedral although few of them ever attended. Quite a number saw little reason to conceal their hostility.

The local greengrocer was particularly vocal in his opposition. Once, when one of the Community women went into his shop and innocently chatted, he let her have his feelings with both barrels. The Community, for its part, struggled with the local culture. Glasgow accents were unintelligible and Americans especially took a long time to read the signals, just as they had done in Coventry. They decided to take the bull by the horns. The local greengrocer was invited to dinner at the Farras' house, and he accepted. It was the beginning of a thaw. Then came the fire, in which 26 people were made homeless. Many of them were housed temporarily in unheated rooms attached to the local

Council offices, known as the Garrison. By the time they left, a big party was thrown for them.

We were still at Yeldall at the time of the fire. Visiting not long afterwards and viewing the blackened ruins, one could sense that in some indefinable way this was a turning point. Things would never be quite the same again.

As it turned out, the fire was the end of the Fisherfolk training ministry. A month or two later the Community held a week long retreat to think about its future. Many people voiced concerns about life on the island and where things were going. At the end of it Jodi Page (now Page-Clark) had a vision or picture of a beautiful flower that closed up and then later burst out again with renewed energy. Visions were common in charismatic circles but this one was memorable because in its details it seemed to catch the essence of the conversation during that retreat.

The move to Cumbrae was a kind of retreat, but it represented more than just a scaling back of ministry commitments. It was a turning point at which Community members, some of whom had joined as students and were now married with children, now had to re-evaluate what community life was about.

Life on the island emphasized their separateness. They were not part of that community. Even in enthusiastic churches it was difficult to see how the Fisherfolk, talented singers and musicians supported by donations, were relevant to the lives of ordinary churchgoers. There was a gut instinct in the Community that what needed to happen was a kind of dying to international stardom and an immersion into everyday life where they were. This was the closing up of the flower. Only then would the real genius of the Community be able to emerge and develop — the opening up of the flower. But what form that would take practically was yet to be seen.

However, it coincided with the need for the Community to generate its own sources of income. One of the first steps was the purchase of the local bakery in Millport. But commercial baking is a specialized business; it took a lot of training and long hours of hard work. Conway Barker and Margi and Bill Pulkingham spent a full year in Glasgow learning the trade. It took a huge amount of commitment and perseverance on their part to enable the Community to run it.

So it was that the international Fisherfolk found themselves working, day in and day out, in routine manual labor. Eventually, after weathering the first day of trading when there was an attempt by some to boycott the shop, they managed to make it into a going concern which was also a useful way to interface with the local people.

Farming was another project. Dave Porter and David Stayner, both part of a Fisherfolk team, headed this one up. Even though David Stayner had been brought up on a farm, there was an enormous amount to learn. There were experiments with goats, pigs, sheep and cows, as well as growing produce. Local farmers may have been inclined to look on with amusement at first, but gave their help when they saw they were serious. The farm was as instrumental as the bakery in helping the Community to integrate with the local people. One couple, Douglas and Christine McDavid, who had been born on the island and were as local as anybody, actually came to work there and began to be involved in the Community's life. At the same time, the businesses provided an occupation for members who needed to be able to work productively.

Yet another project, started a little later, was a guest house. Known as Craig-Ard, this was headed up by Bob and Cathleen Morris. Hospitality seemed to fit in well with the Community's ethos generally and a guest house could be a useful resource for future conference ministry. But the Morrises had almost no experience, and it was extremely hard and exhausting work. Without help it probably would not have been viable, but eventually routines were established that made it into a successful business.

Meanwhile, the business of sorting out corporate identity continued as a kind of backdrop to all this activity. For a while there was an experiment with complete democracy, which multiplied committees and proved an exhausting and unwieldy method of decision making. It was not without its value, in terms of helping individuals to feel more part of things, but it was recognized that many decisions had long term consequences, and the question of who made them was crucial. Not everyone in the Community was there for the long haul, and there had to be some way to ensure that those who were committed long term had control of the direction. There also needed to be an agreed way of dealing with issues such as assets and membership process.

Shortly after the move to Scotland some members had returned to the USA to join with others from Redeemer to establish another Community of Celebration at Woodland Park, high in the Rocky Mountains of Colorado. The purpose of this Community initially was to be the location for business activities previously based in Houston. But it was also a pastoral community. One person who joined had insisted on donating a large sum of money and then later mounted a lawsuit to get it back. The Cumbrae and the Post Green Communities were both named in the suit, and had to find the funds to support Woodland Park. As a result, the newly crafted Community constitution declared that it would not accept money from prospective Community members under any circumstances.

The advice from Nashdom Abbey was that this was probably an overreaction. There were other ways of dealing with the issue, for example Nashdom had arrangements to hold assets in trust until a member died. The Community of Celebration was never wealthy enough to set up that kind of system, but this was all part of the process of laying a foundation for the future of the Community. Another part of that process was engaging in a dialogue with the Church; initially, mainly with the bishops in

Scotland. At that time there were only two options as far as the Anglican Church was concerned: to be either a parish church or a celibate, single sex religious order. The Community hoped to secure recognition as a different form of order. This was the path that Graham felt the Community were on back in the days of Yeldall Manor. He had attended a meeting of Anglican religious chaired by the Bishop of Oxford, Kenneth Woollcombe, who was visitor to some of the orders. He had been invited to present the crux of who the Community were, and chose to paint it as a form of religious order. The bishop told the heads of religious houses that it was up to them. Was this a valid expression of religious life or not? Eventually, after correspondence with the Secretary of the Advisory Council on Relations of Bishops and Religious Communities, the informal advice — wise as it turned out — came back: live with it for 20 years, and then come back to us.

Not everyone thought this direction was the way to go. The late 1970s saw the high water mark of the community movement: by then the Community of Celebration was networking with a number of others. A meeting of international representatives was held at Post Green, which attracted the name "Community of communities." Jim Wallis of the Sojourners Community counseled Graham that to institutionalize his Community in that way would inevitably lead to a loss of charisma. Other voices at that time said the same, including Brian Rice, one of the original trustees of CCCT. "The written code kills, but the Spirit makes alive" (2 Corinthians 3.6). It was a legitimate point of view.

There were risks either way. The Community had always resisted institutionalizing itself, but the problem was that it was possible to go round and round the same circle, asking the same question: what were they? They always felt they needed to retain their family lifestyle. But there was always tension when it came to doing anything creative or specific. It was the tension between the need for change and the need for stability, particularly in the case of families. Following the Spirit was fine, but there needed to be some sort of stable yardstick against which growth and development could happen. The Community was not just a jellyfish, changing shape or form according to whatever the latest contingency happened to be. The Community had begun in a parish church and saw itself as part of and committed to the Anglican Church. From the standpoint of the leadership that meant it had to relate in a way that the Anglican Church could recognize. In the absence of an external framework of authority the likelihood was that the Community would eventually dissipate like a cloud in the sky. Already issues were emerging, such as how decisions were made and who made them, how finances should be dealt with and so on.

Whether things would have turned out differently had the Community chosen to take another direction is hard to say. The Redeemer parish community was never developed into any institutional form, and came to a natural end eventually. Many have suggested that too many gifted leaders were taken away too soon, but church based communities elsewhere did not survive long term either[2].

For the Community of Celebration, however, it was not a question of success in terms of numbers or even in ministry. In the Anglican and Roman Catholic Churches, a small religious community often has an influence out of all proportion to its size. What was important, in the fast moving and largely unstructured period of the 1970s, was to find a stable platform for the future. It was also necessary for a community that included a high proportion of foreign nationals from all over the English speaking world. For better or worse, the Community decided to take the "religious order" route.

1   Kingsway Publications, 1986

2   One interesting development in Britain was the growth of a small Baptist

church in the Northamptonshire village of Bugbrooke, which was inspired by the Redeemer story. It began with a similar sharing of assets and community living and grew into a very large community of some 650 members who formed the nucleus of a series of churches in British cities. Taking the name Jesus Army, they are, as their name suggests, highly mission oriented and disciplined, retaining many of the classic community features typical of Celebration in its earlier years: room sharing, frequent moves, the swap shop, community store and so on. One significant difference is that Baptist churches, being independent, have more flexibility when it comes to structure and ministerial recognition.

Chapter 6

Problems and decline

In terms of record production the peak of activity occurred in the late 1970s, as did the high point in the number of Community members. The top selling Fisherfolk album of all was *Worship with the Fisherfolk*. There was an arrangement between the communities, so that Cumbrae did all the research and development, record production and copyright work, collecting the royalty income, while Post Green was responsible for supplying the trade and collecting sales income. The arrangement worked extremely well. In those days marketing was mainly just a matter of sending out some flyers with a bit of advertizing. Demand was so strong that the records sold themselves.

But things were changing. More commercial Christian music was coming on to the market. The effort needed to sustain a continuous brand of recording was enormous for a community that had other priorities and whose members often moved elsewhere. The rich vein of material that the Community was able to draw on was not inexhaustible, even though there was enough to keep the recording business going for several more years and there were still creative people around to write new songs.

But perhaps one of the most significant events for the future of the recording business was the departure of Betty

Pulkingham. In 1980 Graham returned to Houston together with his household. Betty was not the only competent musician in the Community by any means, but she was the creative driving force. Mimi Farra was extremely talented but was also practical, tempering Betty's enthusiasm and helping to channel it in certain directions. Several other gifted musicians or singers also left or moved elsewhere at around the same time. It did not make it impossible to produce more recordings, but it did take a greater amount of organization and the impetus was not as strong.

There was even a feeling in some quarters that perhaps the business tail was beginning to wag the Community dog. Those who had previously been engaged full time in rehearsal and traveling ministry were now working on the farm or in the bakery.

More generally, fundamental questions were being asked about the vocation of the Community, which in turn caused individuals to examine what their own lives were about. As the years went by, it would become increasingly difficult to sustain business activities by replacing those who moved on.

Graham's departure with his household was a significant blow to the Community. In the tightly knit environment in which people had lived together for years, strong bonds of love had been forged and relationships genuinely were familial, born out of a common commitment and sharing of hardships and joys. The sense of family ties continues to this day amongst many who are now scattered across the world. Graham's move was also a significant reduction in resources. But it was not the loss of leadership that an outside observer might have imagined.

When a meeting was called to tell the Community about the forthcoming move, the group was asked if any one had any questions. Rick Roberts, one of those who had come from Houston, said, "The only question I have is, is Bill staying?" That spoke volumes. It was the clearest possible affirmation of Bill's and Mimi's leadership in the Community. In fact, Graham's position in the Community at this time has been compared to the sidecar of a motorcycle. He was attached to it but not essential to its ongoing life. A younger crop of leadership had emerged who had all lived the same life and made the same moves to Britain and ultimately to Cumbrae. These "second tier" leaders were the kind of solid, dependable people that many a church would envy.

Bill did not object to Graham going back to Houston on the ground that the Community would not make it without him. He was much more concerned about the likelihood of anything positive coming out of his return to Redeemer. Meanwhile, there was another dynamic to deal with. It had been arranged that in Graham's absence Tom and Faith Lees, leaders of the Community at Post Green, would come and spend a year with the Community at Cumbrae.

The purpose of the assignment was to continue integration of the Communities, which had begun with the transfer of Celebration members to Post Green a few years earlier, but in the event it proved a distraction to the process that needed to happen at Cumbrae. They needed to build on what had been achieved since coming to Scotland; the last thing they needed was another round of foundation-laying from a different source.

Communities that look identical on the surface can actually have quite a different ethos at base. Post Green had a particular vision for ministering to wounded people that pre-existed the link with Celebration. It was not as specialized as, say, the L'Arche communities, but it did try to hold a special concern for the weak and vulnerable. That was not incompatible with Celebration as such, but it did affect the way things were approached. In the context of a seasoned group trying to establish a Chapter for its future, it proved to be too confusing to introduce a new and different element.

Tom and Faith's year at Cumbrae did however establish that the two communities had a different ethos, despite sharing many things in common including a similar worship life, virtually interchangeable membership and combined direc-torship of businesses. By this time Post Green had taken the name "The Community of Celebration at Post Green," but it was clear that a lot more work needed to be done if they were to be made one.

After Graham's departure, the Community continued the process of working on structure for the future. By 1980 a provi-sional Chapter had been formed. At Yeldall, authority had resided with a system of elders and pastors inherited from Redeemer. At Cumbrae, there had initially been a group that met to discuss pastoral issues, which included Jerry Barker, a contem-porary of Graham's, who had been such a strong leader at Yeldall. But at Cumbrae he was a support rather than an authority figure distracting the process of Community formation, which involved experiments with democracy and various councils, changing names to make structures feel more appropriate and so on. Bill's leadership style too was different from Graham's. It was less hierarchical, more collegial, more suited to the contemporary culture. It was the kind of leadership needed to create a Chapter, which would be the ultimate decision making body and source of authority.

Not everyone felt able to join the Chapter, which ostensibly meant membership for life although in reality that remained a process for a number of years. (No vows or promises were made at this time.)

To accommodate those unable to make a Chapter commitment, a category of "regular member" was introduced. Some found the concept difficult, given the inclusive "family" nature of community life, but the reasons for it were understood. At around this time a number of people, including some of the most creative and gifted members, decided that community life did not give them enough room to develop. Some left, and one or two others felt they would be better suited to life at Post Green.

Graham's return to Houston was not a huge success. His reasons for going were not altogether clear, but the stated reason was that the parish was still struggling to gain equilibrium after the turmoil surrounding events a few years earlier when Graham resigned. There was something of a power vacuum. The Sunday morning service had been transformed from the community worship of old into a musical showpiece with the choir at its center. For the first year there were some positive signs from Graham's ministry. People were being effectively taught. There were liturgical changes. Guitar leadership was reinvigorated with the "troubadour" style of musicians such as Wiley Beveridge and Richard Gullen. But it was an uphill struggle.

Graham's official role in the parish was that of an assistant priest. From Bill Farra's perspective, that could never work. The idea that a former Rector who had lifted the parish from ashes to international acclaim could come back as an assistant looked absurd; it would have taken a different kind of personality to transform the church.

One of the reasons Graham left Cumbrae was because he was the type of person who always has to dig up the foundation he himself has laid, and he had recognized for a year or so that his presence was a distraction to the formation process there. There were still some elements at Redeemer that wanted him to carry on with the same strength as before, and he may have felt it was an opening for him. But by 1980 the situation had become very different.

Walking around the neighborhood with Graham one day, Bill asked him directly, "Why are you doing this?" But he could see that Graham was not to be dissuaded. Returning to Redeemer was something that, for complex reasons of his own, he really wanted to do. Nevertheless, Bill had never seen him so down in spirits. Graham said something about pressures, and it was obvious that whatever was going on was taking its toll. Soon after that he had a major heart attack, and moved to the Community in Colorado to convalesce.

That was effectively the end of Graham's traveling ministry. He did travel on occasions, but it would be Betty who would now take up the demanding role of tour ministry with the international Fisherfolk team. After a short spell in Colorado, she and Graham returned to England with a group of talented musicians and singers who became the nucleus of a new team, to which others from Cumbrae were added. For a while they were based at Post Green, where there were facilities to rehearse and develop the ministry in isolation, away from the distraction of ongoing life in the communities. When they traveled, Graham became the "at home" person.

In that period of the early 1980s the international team did tours in the USA, Britain, South Africa and Australia. Betty was the spearhead. As a result of the tour in South Africa in 1982 she wrote the *Freedom Mass*, using the songs and rhythms of black South Africa in the apartheid years.

Meanwhile, changes were afoot in Britain. The 1960s and 1970s were a time of optimism and idealism in the community movement, coupled with a degree of naiveté. Lessons had to be learned the hard way on occasion. One example was the Colorado lawsuit, which highlighted the danger of accepting assets from eager prospective Community members. In general the spirit of the times was to travel light, leasing properties rather than buying them, sharing assets with informal agreements that assumed commitment and the spirit of goodwill would carry on forever.

Problems at Redeemer in 1975 showed how fragile this foundation could be. In that situation there was no plan for how to deal with membership and finances over the long term. The ownership of community acquired property operated like a kind of musical chairs. In the exuberance of a dynamic new ministry, it was a matter of indifference as to whose name was on the property deed. People moved around, and for any given household one of its members would be listed as the owner. This didn't matter because everyone was committed to sharing resources and paying the bills, including mortgage payments. Except that it *did* matter, because when the musical chairs stopped the person whose name was on the deed got the title to the property. Someone who had contributed nothing to the purchase of the property could end up owning it. It was a painful if salutary experience for Redeemer.

In Britain, lessons had to be learned too. Major properties such as Yeldall or the cathedral premises at Cumbrae were leased. There were some purchases at Cumbrae, but these were not high value properties and were corporately owned. It was a different story at Post Green, where all the property was privately owned — most, but not all, by the Lees estate. In the spirit of community, it was all shared and made available as the need arose. The merger of Post Green with the Community of Celebration was itself informal, a gentleman's agreement rather than a written contract.

The problems with this arrangement emerged when long term issues of direction began to be addressed. Community members, particularly at Post Green, were a very mixed bunch. Only time would tell who ultimately would adopt community life as their calling, but the more the years went by, the more pressing became the need to settle the issue of property that could provide a stable Community base for the future.

The plan was to link all the Communities of Celebration together in an organization known as the Society of the Community of Celebration. This raised the question of how, apart from the original Community, such a community would be identified. The slightly different ethos at Post Green was already apparent, but the only objective measure was a common constitution that dealt with issues of membership, assets and authority.

Working with these issues produced a kind of paralysis of leadership at Post Green. Eventually, Graham was asked to facilitate a Community retreat at which all the difficulties could be aired. It soon became evident that, although the Community operated in a corporate manner, in the nature of things this could only be a provisional arrangement. Longer term, there would have to be a different foundation than one in which the ministry was based on the Lees family home.

In theory, there was nothing to prevent any particular Community of Celebration from having a specialized ministry. But in reality the historical difference in foundations meant the only way to release the bottleneck was to separate them. The Post Green Community of Celebration would have to be split up so that Post Green itself could pursue its original goals in the way that it needed to. For the Celebration element there it meant either disbanding or moving somewhere else.

The effect of these conclusions was cataclysmic for many of those involved. Since the move from Yeldall individuals from the two original communities had intermingled and formed strong and lasting relationships. Some were happy with the emphasis on healing of the wounded, while others did not understand their vocation in that specific way. Some had resources and could make adjustments relatively easily, while others had burned their boats and were facing an uncertain future, particularly as Cumbrae could not provide a place for all those potentially displaced.

Cumbrae, too, was facing its own form of crisis during this time. The 10 year lease on the Cathedral property ran out in 1985, and the trustees did not seem disposed to renew it. The Community were now looking to own rather than lease property in future. Although they did own some property on Cumbrae, without the Cathedral and the college there was no focus for their ministry. The prospect of moving was raised here too.

The effect of all this in the mid 1980s was like shaking a tree full of fruit. Large numbers of Community members decided it was time to move on with their lives. Most of these were at Post Green but Cumbrae was affected too. Many were foreign nationals who returned to their own country. Many were people who had joined in their twenties and were now in their thirties, needing to decide what their lives were about. At Post Green, a smaller group identified itself as a Community of Celebration while a similar group became a community for the original vision of Post Green. The Woodland Park Community, which had seen a number of its members move to Britain to become part of the international Fisherfolk team, also came to a natural end in 1985 and disbanded. It was the end of an era for the big communities.

In retrospect, although at the time it seemed a huge upheaval, the reduction in numbers would almost certainly have happened anyway in the course of time. It was inevitable that younger members and foreign nationals would need to seriously review their future at some point. But more than that, the times themselves were changing. The Thatcher–Reagan years created a totally different climate. Yuppies, the young upwardly mobile, were the icons of the day, and the church was affected like every other sector of society. People were not flocking to join community any more. Christian music was changing too. It was becoming more commercial, more performance oriented. The folk idiom was passé. By 1980, even the Fountain Trust had closed. Big national events such as Spring Harvest, later to be followed by New Wine, were becoming the main focus of church renewal in Britain.

Meanwhile, the concentration on constitutional matters and membership process was bringing the Community of Celebration to where it needed to be. For its own future, it needed to establish the core who understood it as their life vocation. It looked as if it would be a smaller group than the Community were used to in the past. But it would also be easier to work with.

Chapter 7

Relocation

Initially members of the Community of Celebration were not thinking of returning to the USA. The plan was to relocate to somewhere in mainland Britain. Their first thought was to return to their roots in the inner city, for which there was plenty of scope in Scotland. They received no feelers from England, but the Bishop of Brechin, Ted Luscombe — soon to be appointed Primus — visited the Community and talked about Dundee, where he was based. That was certainly an urban situation.

Relations with their own bishop, the successor to Richard Wimbush who had been so supportive in inviting them to the island, were not easy at this time, and he was chairman of the cathedral trustees. On reflection, they realized that one of the main things that had happened as a result of living on the island was that they had had the space to develop a constitution and make a start on becoming formed as a kind of Benedictine community. It had allowed a consciousness to develop of who they were. Now, having done that, what was the future for living on the island? They would have had to become more contemplative and possibly even monastic. Yet they still had sensibilities about ministry. They felt they were not yet done as far as parish renewal was concerned.

From a lifestyle point of view most of the Community were quite happy and would have stayed there. The idea of raising children in a more natural way was appealing. But that was not the point on which they felt they needed to focus. However valid in its own right, it was not the kind of vision that would feed them. What nurtured them at a spiritual level was a vision of renewal of the worshiping life of the people of God. They had certainly experienced this at Cumbrae, in sharing with the local people, as a letter from Christine McDavid, written in retrospect, shows.

"Looking back to their years on Cumbrae," she wrote, "[the Community of Celebration] gave me the real meaning of why Jesus Christ came into the world — love, care, friendship, worship and prayer. The times I remember more than any were the 'family gathering.' Simple songs, sharing cares and concerns, giving thanks to the Lord for his help and guidance in our daily lives, bread and wine passed from one to another, and then after that time the pot luck supper—it was wonderful. There were lots of services, shared work and help, gardening, love and care for the flowers and animals. I give thanks to the Lord for bringing the C. of C. to the Island of Cumbrae. I am as close to them now as then, and we are all close in the Holy Spirit."

But without the Cathedral and a supportive ecclesial environment it was difficult to see how the vision for renewal of the worshiping life of the church could be maintained, let alone developed. This was a concern of the Community as a whole, but for Bill Farra it also had a more personal aspect.

Having left Cumbrae a few years previously and now finding themselves back in England with another group that constituted the international Fisherfolk team, Betty and Graham were trying to work with "the fourth community" as it was known, which was based at Post Green. But it was not easy for them. The age difference was as much as 30 years, and even the addition of others from Cumbrae could not bridge the generation gap. In fact, ever since Graham's spell back at the Church of the Redeemer, Bill felt that he did not do too well in community life without Bill himself being around somewhere. Graham talked about moving to Florida, but Bill could see that that would be a failure without someone like himself, capable of standing up to him with the gifts to facilitate moving things along.

So in addition to Community discussions there were also personal conversations along the lines of "we were wondering about our future and your future." Bill did not think the international team had a future as things stood. So it came about that the "fourth community" together with Graham and Betty joined their future to that of the Cumbrae Community in 1983/4. They seriously considered Dundee. But the proposed location was a desperate place. It was a housing estate where the property was very old and full of mildew. Many properties were left vacant.

In 1984, Betty and the international team went through the Pittsburgh area on a ministry tour. Anna Hathaway, wife of the Bishop of Pittsburgh, was quite a fan of the Fisherfolk. The Bishop himself, Alden Hathaway, had also had some contact through "renewal" mornings. The Community had made it a point not to noise abroad the fact that they were looking to relocate, but they got a message from Alden Hathaway saying he understood they wanted to move and suggested they come to his diocese. How he knew was a mystery.

The Community had drawn up a list of criteria for the place they would eventually settle in. Pittsburgh certainly met one of those, a favorable ecclesial environment. In the USA Destin Florida was another place considered, but that hardly met the criterion of a place in real need.

Other criteria included a place where they could have both common life and household living without being spread over too wide an area. They wanted to be close to an international airport, as they thought they would still be able to travel. They wanted to have access to institutions of higher learning. They needed an environment that looked as if it would enable them to support themselves and earn a living. They also wanted to be near a church that was functional and not dependent on them as had been the case during their ten years at the cathedral.

A possible site in the city of Aliquippa seemed to meet most of these criteria. A steel town some 20 miles outside Pittsburgh, this was a place seriously threatened by the disappearance of its only industry. A block of property was available close to its center. It was a quick run to Pittsburgh airport. The Episcopal Church of All Saints was almost next door and seemed lively enough. One of the national ECUSA seminaries, Trinity Episcopal School for Ministry, was not far away, just across the Ohio River. So the decision was made. The Community felt a bit like the Israelites leaving Egypt and going out into the unknown, albeit with an optimistic spirit.

It was at this point that some decided that going to western Pennsylvania was not what they were called to do. Some returned to the USA; others went south to Post Green or did other things. It was not out of disillusionment with Community life; it came more from the feeling of some individuals that this was not a direction they needed to take. Some advisers told the Community they needed to do proper fund raising. A friend who was a professional fund raiser actually came to live in the Community for a year. But it was not much of a success when the costs were taken into account. Most of the funding came from donors who would have given money anyway; Community supporters were very faithful. To this day the Community has never found professional fund raising techniques helpful.

Meanwhile the group at Post Green who had decided they wanted to continue as a Community of Celebration were trying to establish their own corporate identity. It was a confusing time. Since there had been only been one joint ministry in the past, it was not clear how much of the old would carry over to the new. This applied not only to ministry but also to the support base. There was only one mailing list, for example, which now had to decide whether it wanted to receive newsletters from both groups, only one or neither. There were many issues to sort out, such as the division of office equipment and goods and chattels. Certain matters, particularly tenure of property, the ownership of copyrights and establishment of another charity, made it essential to establish separate legal representation.

From our point of view, having moved from Yeldall to Post Green, it was an extremely testing time. Remaining where we were meant effectively starting family life again from scratch, yet pursuing our original calling meant taking on the responsibility of starting a new community without any of the resources that the earlier international ministry could attract. There were risks either way. In the end calling won out, and for better or worse we decided to give ourselves to the project of continuing a Community of Celebration presence in England.

Not least among the problems to sort out were the questions of location and the future support base. It was clearly impossible to simply carry on independently at the same spot. Any new location would minimally require housing and a place to meet. Those who constituted the new community were self selecting; it was not a group put together by careful planning about its future needs. It had virtually nothing in the way of personal financial resources and it was obvious that ministry alone could not support it. The only viable option was for individuals to secure employment. That was easier said than done, given that everyone had been full time in community life for years and the place where they would ultimately settle was unknown at this stage.

Feelers were put out to the Bishops of Liverpool, Birmingham and Southwark (south London), which led to meetings with them or their representatives. All were favorable, but the Bishop of Southwark, Ronnie Bowlby, was particularly warm in his response and tried to secure a large property connected to a church. Unfortunately this fell foul of the trustees, and the Community were left in an emergency situation as the agreed tenure of their property at Post Green expired in 18 months. By this time there were only a few months left to go.

When the Community at Cumbrae moved to the USA, a question had arisen as to what should happen to CCCT, the charity set up in the early 1970s to support the Community of Celebration. Members of the group at Post Green were brought on to the management committee, and CCCT became the vehicle that supported the ongoing work in England. It made it possible both to attract donations and to hold major assets in common. Through friends of the Community, discussions were held with the South Park Community Trust, a Christian charity that owned a large property in the village of Bletchingley to the south of London but still within the Southwark Diocese.

The South Park Community Trust was empowered by its constitution to sell property at less than the full market price to another charity. The property at Bletchingley, known as Berry House, was sold to CCCT. Despite the price advantage it was a very large sum. It required a bank loan, for which individual Community members were personally liable. The Community did the sums and believed that they could do it, but it would take a lot of commitment and would be very much a faith venture.

Bletchingley, which derives its ancient name from "bleaching lye" as a result of mineral quarrying in the area, is only a short run to London's Gatwick Airport. British Airways ran a direct flight from there to Pittsburgh, which made travel between the Communities easy and convenient. The way was now open for the two remaining Communities in the USA and Britain to establish links through the structure devised earlier, the Society of the Community of Celebration.

Thus the mid-1980s was effectively a watershed time for the Community of Celebration. Prior to 1985 there had been three or four large communities with an extensive ministry. After that year there were just two much smaller communities in completely new locations, both of them preoccupied with the need to establish a long term stable base. Both were acutely conscious of their roots. But from this point on, "following the Spirit" would have a new meaning. The old happy go lucky days of constant changes and impermanent locations were over.

Chapter 8

The Making of the Modern Community

Compared to Britain, property in downtown Aliquippa was very cheap. An entire block of houses was bought from a slum landlord. They were in a very poor condition and needed major renovation work. Through loans and donations the Community were also able to acquire several other properties: a former funeral home, a former Presbyterian church, now closed, together with its manse. All of this was very close together, thereby fulfilling one of the criteria for moving, that it should be a site that made it possible for Community life to exist without being too dispersed.

But another of the major criteria fell apart at the seams almost as soon as the Community arrived. From their experience at Cumbrae, the Community was determined that it did not want to be responsible for the running of a parish. Parish life is demanding and presents too many distractions for a community trying to understand its ministry and establish its identity as a form of religious order. The Community had been told that the nearby All Saints Episcopal church was active and had a viable life of its own. The vision was that Community and church would be working together as independent bodies in the mission to the town.

In fact, two priests from the parish church disappeared within three months of the arrival of the Community. A plan was in motion to build a church out in the suburbs where many of the congregation lived, the idea being to divide the church on a 50-50 basis with the combined parish being managed by the existing Rector of All Saints. The Community were aware of this, but what had not been communicated was that the Rector had already accepted a call to another parish. It was clear that this had been known for some time. The sudden loss of leadership resulted in a joint parish in two vastly different places, one of which now looked as if it was about to become a lame duck. The Community could not escape the feeling that the locals had seen them coming.

At this stage it was important for the Community that there be an Episcopal Church presence nearby. They had their roots in a parish church and were concerned about local church renewal. As expected, however, the combined parish idea proved unworkable and was abandoned after a couple of years. All Saints would probably have closed at that point, but Graham came up with a plan to establish the Community as a "corporate rector." Rather than have a priest from the Community take responsibility for the church as a full time job, the ministry would be shared. It was accepted by the diocese, but the future of the church looked uncertain and it would be a drain on the Community.

America proved a culture shock for all those who came from Britain, including the Americans themselves. They had been gone from the country for 13 years. During that time changes had taken place in all of them as individuals, but their corporate lifestyle had also changed through 10 years on a Scottish island. It had become more basic and interdependent. The pace was a lot slower and life was hard. Western Pennsylvania was as typically American as anywhere else, but it also included a strong stable ethnic mix. The public schools were very different from Scotland; the Community had to adjust to a culture based on cars and conveniences, and so on.

The one time Presbyterian Church building was known as the Celebration Center. Initially the idea was that this was to be the focus of the Community's ministry, which would include conferences and a training institute. It would also be a place for the Community to worship. They tried it for a while, but it soon became evident that the building was high on maintenance and needed a lot done to it. Among other issues there were problems with asbestos. It was eventually sold, but there continued to be a long term problem of a place to meet. The Community was too big for the rooms at the office and All Saints Church was primarily a place to attend on Sunday, though the Community did hold its daily prayers there.

Despite the Community's reluctance to take on responsibility for a church, the vision of a ministry of parish renewal remained an active one at this stage. Graham adopted ideas from a program of parish renewal involving leadership training that had some currency at the time. Notwithstanding the space problem he had not given up on the idea of training; in fact, one of his reasons for suggesting that the Community take on responsibility for All Saints Church was that to talk about parish renewal there needed to be a working model of it. He continued to do some traveling as a conference speaker, but the reality of All Saints was that its problems were terminal, even though the Community would continue propping it up for a number of years. The changes that happened just as the Community arrived had taken away all of its leadership and 80% of its congregation, so there was nowhere to go with it. "Have a good time by yourselves" seemed to be the attitude of those who had chosen to move away.

It is possible that Graham at this time was trying to make some sense of his own past. It would have been natural, but the fact was that All Saints was a very different proposition from the Church of the Redeemer and everyone, not least Graham himself, had changed as a result of the hard pioneering work of establishing a religious community. There were some in the Community who felt the past as something of a burden and wanted to put away delusions of grandeur. Not everyone necessarily thought the same, but the vision for that type of conference and training ministry was gradually coming to an end.

The Community numbered some 35 people at this stage. Some of those who came from Britain did not commit to full membership but lived close by and participated in its life. Others joined from various places (including Houston) and lived in the row houses. Some were local people, attracted by the worship at All Saints. Some came from more distant places to experience community life. Some were seminarians at TESM, the Episcopal school at Ambridge just across the river. One way or another, there always seemed to be plenty of people around, living on the property or nearby, who all contributed to the Community's life.

The majority of these said they wanted to pursue membership, which involved entering as a novice, moving to provisional Chapter status and finally to life vowed membership of the Chapter. One such example was Dennis Wilson, who joined the membership process but later realized that his family commitments would prevent him from becoming a full member. However, he wanted to stay involved so continued to live in one of the row houses, working in the Community accounts department. That was a track followed by a number of others. Gradually a pattern emerged. People would come, pursue membership and eventually decide that it wasn't for them—yet often wanted to stay involved. Others arrived who were looking to change their life direction, but without destroying everything they had been a part of in the past. Often these were gifted people who made a substantial contribution to the Community's life and ministry.

Typically these individuals would stay for about three years and then move on. After a while, the Community realized that it was becoming a safe haven for certain people who were at a genuine crossroads in their life, unsure what their future path would be. Rather than seeing someone's departure as a failure because they didn't stay the course, this came to be seen as a legitimate ministry. The Community provided a place of stability, so that the pursuit of membership became the channel for people to follow their own process of discovering what their lives were about.

Those who had been involved in the Community's life in Britain were part of the furniture, so to speak — yet they too were in a personal process of discovery. Younger members particularly were facing into life issues such as the possibilities of marriage or choice of career. The Community sent three of its members to train as priests, and another was later ordained after leaving to pursue an academic track. All of these were very successful in their subsequent careers. Others were facing similar choices, which took time to emerge at Aliquippa, despite often having lived in community for many years. The Community was "home"; it offered a viable life path in itself, yet for some who had known little else as adults there was also a need to leave home. The depth and quality of relationships in community would remain, and would form the basis of an ongoing network of friends scattered around the world.

Back in Scotland, the McKeown family had joined the Community but was unable to immigrate to the USA because of a visa delay. In the meantime, Steven McKeown had become ordained as a deacon. When the visas finally arrived, the family moved to Aliquippa and Steven pursued ordination as a priest in the Episcopal Church, thereby enabling him to serve the needs at All Saints as well as the Community. Barbara Gilbert took a masters degree and got a job teaching at the local school. Mimi Farra took a post at Trinity Episcopal School for Ministry (TESM), teaching music and liturgy. Gradually, Community members were beginning to settle into who they were as people, and for some of them that would mean employment at

Aliquippa. It also meant that the Community was now beginning to penetrate the fabric of the town.

After about three years at Aliquippa the Community instituted an Order of Companions. Modeled on the Benedictine system of oblates, it involved a simple Rule that each could adapt to their own circumstances and encouraged a regular visit to the Community. The Community's support base had been asking for something like this for years. There were many people who were genuinely committed to the Community; they saw themselves as more than regular donors or visitors, yet they would never be able to join. There needed to be some way to recognize their commitment. The Order of Companions was a loose but significant way of recognizing people who supported the Community in a variety of ways. Sometimes former members also saw it as a way to continue their relationship. At the initial induction service, there were 57 people.

In parallel with this, the Community of Celebration established in England also formed its own Order of Companions. As most members of that Community held full time jobs, a significant element of the Community's ministry came to be the regular weekend day conferences for Companions and their families, calling for creativity in worship and activities as well as a teaching ministry. The two Communities kept in regular touch through exchange visits by those free enough to do it, thereby ensuring that within the Society of the Community of Celebration there was a broadly similar ethos. One of the enduring ministries of the Aliquippa Community was an annual summer residential Companions conference, which proved to be an ideal opportunity for members of the English Community to visit and then stay on to exchange ideas.

In addition to a constitution, the Community began to evolve a Rule of Life after the move to Pennsylvania. In the early days at Yeldall Manor, they had often referred to themselves as a "lifestyle" community as opposed to a "rule of life" community, the implication being that their life was much more flexible, family oriented, "following the Spirit." However, as long term issues such as membership and authority for decisions began to emerge, it had become clear that some form of institutional structure would be necessary to secure a long term future, including a description of Celebration's own distinctive ethos.

The Benedictine Rule was chosen as a model, because it offered the most flexibility and the best chance of incorporating the needs of families.

It was understood that "rule" did not mean a law that had to be obeyed. It was simply a description of how life worked in the Community "as a rule." The life did have features to it that were identifiable and often commented on by visitors. There were things that new members needed to learn if they were going to stay long term. But the Rule was a different type of document from a constitution. It was something that needed to be studied, reflected on and perhaps experimented with. It was not an inflexible document imposed from the top down; it had to be owned by the Community as a whole and be capable of development as times and needs changed.

There were two aspects to developing a Rule, writing it and working with its provisions. Graham was involved in both. One example of an experiment was the institution of a time of confession in conjunction with daily worship. It served a good purpose for a time, encouraging people to be open and vulnerable and not complaining, but after a while it seemed to have fulfilled its function and was not included in the Rule. Although Graham wrote the initial draft, his language did not necessarily reflect that of the Community as a whole, who needed to make the Rule their own. Working with the Rule was a constant process, which included the Community in England.

The mission of the Community was simply to be a presence, or to put it in the words of the constitution, "to be a sign of the celebration of life in Jesus Christ, and a friend of the poor and oppressed." The Community saw itself as an encouragement to the neighborhood and a welcoming presence for any who happened to visit. Local initiatives and agencies were supported, such as the Aliquippa Alliance which tried to attract new business to the town. Individual Community members were involved locally through their work. But in terms of everyday Community life, for a number of years there were perhaps three main preoccupations.

The first was All Saints church, which was quite a drain. Graham had oversight of the "corporate rector" concept, and anything that he was involved in usually took a lot of resources. Many Community members were involved in that ministry over a number of years.

Secondly, the demands of ordinary life were heavy, particularly in the initial stages. The renovation and refurbishment of the properties was a major project, as was the need to achieve economic stability. There were also environmental issues, not unrelated to the overall mission. The property needed to be well presented, to counter the impression of decay in the locality. The back yard area was converted into a pleasant stretch of grass, secluded from the main street and bordered with trees and plants. Out front, the old broken sidewalk was re-laid.

The third preoccupation was research and development, which continued from the Cumbrae days. The songbooks published in Britain, *Songs from Sound of Living Waters*, *Songs from Fresh Sounds* and *Cry Hosanna* were now out of print. *Come Celebrate!* was a new project, designed as a supplement to the American Episcopal Hymnal published in 1982. It contained many of the songs previously published as well as fresh material. But there was also more to it than a songbook. Part of the package offered by the Community was a *Come Celebrate!* weekend, at which churches would receive teaching on how to use it. Betty Pulkingham continued to travel with former members of the Fisherfolk on this type of ministry for a number of years.

In 1992 an event occurred that shook the Community to its foundations. A complaint was lodged against Graham about the conduct of a pastoral relationship. A journalist got hold of the story, and the reverberations went round the world, for Graham was a significant figure in charismatic church circles. Within the Community it was difficult to know how to deal with it, because Graham was such a big person even though he was no longer the dominant force that he had been. There was a lot of anger and fear at what was felt as a betrayal.

Although Graham wanted to meet with the Community to apologize, younger members were afraid that he might use his powers of rationalization to win them over or paint a different picture of what had happened. Others thought such a meeting would be much the best thing and a better path towards health, yet for the sake of the Community as a whole felt they had to set that aside. It was an extremely painful time for everyone. Eventually it was agreed that Graham and Betty would withdraw from the Community in the hope and expectation of reconciliation once the dust had settled.

It was not to be. Before an investigation could be completed, Graham died. The manner of his death seemed in keeping with the man. He and Betty were in a supermarket when the disgruntled boy friend of a female employee came in and started firing a gun. True to form, Graham started walking towards the commotion rather than away from it, and as he did so he suffered a massive heart attack that left him in a coma. Doctors advised that he had no chance of recovery, and a couple of weeks later he died. But his funeral in North Carolina *was* a witness to reconciliation. It was a powerful occasion attended by a large number of friends including Community members from Aliquippa and from England.

Graham was an extraordinary man by anybody's standards. Without him, the Church of the Redeemer in Houston would probably have closed in the 1960s and the Community of

Celebration would never have happened. His partnership with Betty led to a form of spiritual renewal in the church that spread its influence across the globe.

In worship, the music that came out of the shared, common life of the communities filled songbooks and recordings that sold in hundreds of thousands — much of which is still in use today. None of this would have been possible had not Graham opened his heart to God to see what the Spirit would do some 30 years earlier.

He was a complex man. Frank Lake told a story of how he and Graham once took an in depth psychological test and discovered that both their personalities scored high on the psychopathic scale. Maybe that is what is required of charismatic leaders: the ability to push a project through despite obstacles. He could be hard on those whose attitudes or behavior he judged to be in contravention of the spirit of the life, and some were afraid of him. But he also had enormous compassion for the weak, the vulnerable and the poor, and if you were ever hugged by him you knew you had been hugged by a man. He was the essential priest, a person who affirmed people in their identity and got them to believe in God.

Although he did a lot of teaching over the years, most of it was pastoral rather than in the form of theological analysis, and this may have been one reason why he seemed reluctant to write a theological book despite being widely read himself. His own theology was influenced by the writings of E.P. Mascall, one of which, *The Importance of Being Human*, had a special resonance for community life. This may well have helped to shape the Community's own understanding of spiritual life at a time when "renewal" in the church at large often seemed to lead to a one-sided focus on the divine.

The "religious order" concept was in large measure Graham's own. He was looking for some way to make what had happened at Redeemer permanent. Whatever form that took, for him it had to be a valid form of church—a form that the institutional church could recognize—as opposed to being a para-church agency. The vision was for the renewal of the church: not just the spiritual life of some of its members but also its structures. That required some form of institutional expression that was itself part of the structure, and for Graham, being an Anglican, that meant a religious order.

Once established, however, much of the work of developing it had to be done by the members themselves. Graham would not have been the first founder to find it difficult to live in the institution he founded. He needed new challenges, but his heart attack in 1981 was a clear warning. He could no longer give himself to ministry with the energy that he had once had, and his eventually fatal heart attack (though probably induced by stress) was in a way an event waiting to happen.

Was Graham a prophet, as many have described him? There is no doubt that he was a compassionate and complex man, with a flamboyant personality, who had been through some very deep waters in his own life. It may still be too soon to be objective, but some have suggested an analogy from Martin Luther King jnr., who was a Baptist minister and a towering figure in the Civil Rights movement yet was known to have feet of clay. The impact that Martin Luther King had is undeniable, despite a different side to his life. So with Graham: what was achieved by him and through him is not negated by *his* feet of clay—but feet of clay are, nevertheless, part of his story.

After his death things changed in a number of ways. Several people left, although the reasons were more complex and personal than a simple cause and effect. Following Betty's departure, the *Come Celebrate!* ministry had lost its main driver and began to be less prominent, though it still continued for several years. The Community entered a period of reflection and introspection, which included working on the Rule of Life with the Community in England.

In England, the core of the Community consisted of three Chapter couples, Gordon and Susan Abbott, Phil and Margaret Bradshaw and Stephen and Lorna Ball, together with their families. The Abbotts had come from Houston, via Cumbrae and Post Green, where Susan had a gifted counseling ministry. The Bradshaws had joined the Community at Yeldall Manor, later transferring to Post Green, and the Balls were the adult children of families that were part of the original (pre-Celebration) community at Post Green. It was a good mix, later joined by a number of new members.

Susan and Phil normally represented their Community at inter-community meetings, with one other member where possible. In these discussions ideas began to form on the subject of vows. Although the process was that more recent members made promises at certain points, full chapter membership consisted of self-selecting members from the pre-1985 era who were trying to establish their community for the long term but had never actually taken vows themselves. For them, just being there for a couple of decades constituted their membership process. Now, the question of recognition was beginning to surface again. The 20 years they had once been told to wait was not yet up, but if recognition was going to happen it would require formal life vows in the presence of an official representative of the church.

Traditional monastic vows are vows of poverty, chastity and obedience, but these were not considered suitable for a community that included married couples. The Benedictine approach was less stringent and allowed greater flexibility. Thus in Celebration's case the wording promised stability, conversion of life and obedience in the service of the Community, according to the Rule. Stability in particular was a new concept at first, but its relevance was obvious given the Community's history.

"Following the Spirit" made for an extraordinarily dynamic life, but it was also inherently unstable, with constant change and many comings and goings. Even in the early days questions were being asked as to who would be in it for the long haul—an aspect of stability necessary for the founding of a permanent community. Another aspect was the willingness to hang in with relationships. The vows did not stand in isolation; they were to be undertaken in the context of the Community's Rule.

Strange as it seemed, it was still not clear who would actually take such vows. Quite a few of those remaining from pre-1985 days had already decided that in the long term their future lives would need to take a different track. In the end, just 12 people from both communities put themselves forward to make life vows, including four Chapter members in England.

This was not the sum total of Community members, but it was the permanent core that hopefully would continue and be joined by others. Basil Matthews OSB, then Abbot of Elmore Abbey near Newbury in England, was asked to receive the vows at a ceremony that took place on July 27 1996 in All Saints Church Aliquippa. From the Community's point of view, the goal they had been working towards ever since the first pioneers had arrived in Britain from Houston had now been achieved.

Chapter 9

Community in the 21st century

Basil Matthews, a man of many years experience of religious communities, warned that life vows did not necessarily mean that no-one would leave or that things would always stay the same. So it proved. Within a few years, for a variety of reasons including illness and death, the original core group of twelve life vowed members were reduced to eight. These changes included the closure of the English Community, which did not have the resources to meet the challenges of maintaining an independent community. Remaining life vowed members attached themselves to the Aliquippa Community and what was ultimately established in England was a "Celebration house" maintained by one couple, an arrangement that continues to this day.

Meanwhile at Aliquippa the ministry at All Saints also came to a close. It had been clear for a long time that the church only survived because the Community was propping it up. The diocese concluded that it was no longer viable and decided to close it. The building was subsequently used for a time by the Church Army, a development that proved fruitful in a different way for the Community.

The final service at All Saints at Easter 1999 was a kind of waymark, indicating the end of a 14 year era not only of parish ministry but also roughly the same period of traveling ministry in the USA. By the late 1990s much of what the *Come Celebrate!* weekends had to offer had been absorbed by the church. Since these were also linked to parish renewal, the closure of All Saints generated a feeling that the weekends were talking about things that were not really coming out of the Community's life as it was now. It also renewed a long-standing issue about what the Community's role and function was.

The original vision had been for a community that was *alongside* a parish. Despite their unusual lifestyle, there had been no sense that the Community was an *alternative* to a parish. Although the Community had a worship life of its own, its members had always attended the local church. So when All Saints closed, the question was, what would the Community do? Would they not attend Sunday worship? It was clear that the Community would still seek to be involved in some way at the level of a local church, because that had always been part of their fabric.

But it also had the ethos of worship where you lived. It was always possible to drive past other churches to one that suited best, but that was not really what they were about. It had always been about being church where you were.

The closure of All Saints brought this issue up in stark relief. Was the Community going to find a suitable church to worship in, or was it going to continue where they were even though technically there was no parish? The decision was to keep on worshiping where they were.

It was a point in time when they had to refigure their reason for being. They were not tending to a parish. They were no longer traveling and trying to renew the church at parish level. So what were they trying to do? In the end it was decided that they were trying to be a Christian presence in their own neighborhood. They had a ministry of hospitality. They wanted people to come and experience their worship ministry rather than sending teams out to recreate it. This was a significant shift in consciousness, for in the past, ever since Houston days, the ministry had always been about encouraging parish renewal in the church at large. Now, that was no longer the case.

Nevertheless, the Community did not see themselves as a parish. Instead, they spoke in terms of a ministry of presence. That expression arose because of the question commonly asked, "What do you do? What's your program?" Ultimately the answer was that the Community did whatever came to hand. If someone returned after visiting 10 years previously they would say, "This is not what I remember. This is not the Community of Celebration that I knew. There are different activities."

Yet the Community *was* the same, in all essentials. The ministry of presence was not a cop out — saying "we really don't have anything to do, so we're just being a presence" — but if people insisted that the Community justified its existence by means of a program, then that program was "being" — making the life available to whoever happened to be there at the time.

Obviously that changed as needs changed or people changed, but the principle of a Christian presence remained the same. It was a hard concept for some to grasp.

Looking back, it was clear that institutionalizing the Community with a constitution had been a big issue for some. Many individuals joined the Community over the years who were self motivated and ministry oriented people. What they were good at (and known for) was getting stuck in and getting things done. When such individuals were hampered by corporate life, it changed their experience of ministry. In normal circumstances, the way to proceed was to decide what needed to happen. There might be some negotiation with others, but essentially it was a matter of certain individuals making a decision and then getting on and doing it. In that context, a life that required openness to others and hearing God together could well be experienced as a frustrating distraction.

In this situation some people might well say, "I don't want to be limited by all this; I just want to do what the Spirit says." But in fact "what the Spirit says" in a corporate context is different from an individual one. Neither is better than the other, necessarily; but they are different.

Looking at it a little simplistically, over the space of 35 years or so the Community changed its focus and its location several times. Membership, too, changed as people joined or transferred from other places. At each of these transitions there was always a certain percentage who would say, "This is a different community; this is not what I joined. When I joined, we were all about such and such an activity, and that's where my gifts are." Moving from the south of England to the Scottish island of Cumbrae was one such junction. When the Community began talking about membership process and long term commitment, that was another cause for fall out. Some felt that the community they joined was all about music and the arts, so talk of commitment and the long haul was not for them.

It was a similar story at Aliquippa. As the Community became less glamorous or spectacular in its forms of ministry, there were some who felt they needed to be part of something bigger, where their gifts could shine. It was a legitimate point of view, but what was left ultimately was a group of people who certainly had gifts — outstanding ones in some respects — yet with an underlying commitment to the process of following the Spirit together, using gifts for the common good whatever that happened to be. It was not unlike a marriage. In a marriage, things often had to change. One partner might say that a given situation did not work for them, so the other partner would pick up responsibilities and compensate. There was always the choice of splitting up, of saying, for instance, "I didn't marry you believing I would have to look after a paraplegic for the rest of my life." Or you could adapt.

The Community that remained were the adapters. Many others took a different view. At times of transition there had often been a feeling of people leaving a sinking ship. Some who had left even encouraged those remaining to leave, saying "You can survive. There is a life outside community. You are not dependent on it." Of course that was true, even though life prospects diminished the longer people stayed. But most people were not in it because of dependency.

Whether they left or stayed, for the vast majority it was a matter of understanding their calling, or at least what their lives needed to be about.

By early 2001 the national Episcopal Church agreed to formally recognize the Community of Celebration under the canons governing religious communities. Its first Visitor under this new regime was Bishop Bill Folwell. The next step was to construct a purpose built chapel. Space was available behind the office block, and an architect who happened to be one of the Community Companions was commissioned. He designed a complex that included a chapel and a kitchen, dining and sitting area built on to the existing office, creating a single indoor area. It took two years to build and was dedicated at a special service in August 2003 attended by a large number of former Community members, Companions and other friends.

It is hard to overestimate the significance of the chapel, which symbolically represented the culmination of a journey of "following the Spirit" that had begun in Houston decades earlier. The journey had involved hundreds of people and two continents, not to mention traveling all over the English speaking world. Its name chose itself: it was dedicated as the Chapel of the Holy Spirit.

For the Community, the chapel changed things profoundly. It was not so much a visible change — people were not flocking to worship with the Fisherfolk — but it meant that the Community now had a place to be hospitable and a set apart worship space which was versatile enough to provide for a variety of functions.

It made it possible to host teaching sessions or conferences as the need arose, or simply to be hospitable to the wide variety of guests who were coming and going all the year round. In retro-spect, the closure of All Saints now felt like a blessing in disguise.

Gradually, the ministry of presence began to develop, though not perhaps in quite the way that earlier pioneers had expected. The importance of "presence" had always been felt—for example, penetrating the neighborhood through employment, or offering low cost housing to people with a poor credit rating — but there had always been other preoccupations that took a lot of human resources, which in turn grew harder to sustain as numbers reduced.

Once the chapel was built, however, instead of growing in numbers to expand its ministry of presence, the Community and its plant seemed to act like a magnet for other individuals and agencies that had the resources for ministry in the town. The Community was able to offer housing, office space and a place of worship and fellowship.

The Church Army presence that replaced All Saints was a significant injection of energy into the local situation, involving partnership with the Community in a variety of ways. Other agencies followed. A former Community member bought the one-time Salvation Army building next door to the office and made it available to the Community, greatly increasing the facilities. In one way or another all these connections led to a congregation at Community worship that ebbed and flowed according to whether people were at home or out of town. During the summer the number of guests increased. Conference ministry was now possible on site instead of having to hire premises elsewhere. Summer workers (mainly young people) came to work with one or other of the mission agencies. A regular Taizé service attracted a different congregation, including a number of local people.

The chapel thus represented a functional improvement but perhaps the deepest change was what it meant in terms of identity. The old question, what exactly *is* the Community, had finally been laid to rest. It was not an intentional parish, because it was self contained and self sufficient. It was a worshiping community, but the chapel added something. It facilitated worship in a variety of ways, but above all it confirmed the Community in its identity as an ecclesial happening. It made it possible both for the Community itself and for others to understand it as a legitimate form of church, in much the same way that monastic orders are recognized.

II ASPECTS OF COMMUNITY LIFE

Chapter 10

Worship

The origins of the worship for which the Fisherfolk became famous go all the way back to the times of worship and praise held by the small group in Houston who met daily for up to three hours to share their lives in the context of praise. Later this developed into a distinctive folk style in a coffee house ministry.

In those days coffee house ministry was ground breaking. Known as The Way Inn, this was an outreach of the Church of the Redeemer to the drug and hippie culture of the day, and was essentially a youth ministry.

One of the people drawn in by this ministry was Mikel Kennedy, an ex-drug addict who found healing in the Redeemer community and later came to Britain as a member of the Fisherfolk. He was a talented musician, whose songs such as *Never in My Life* and *Isn't it Good?* (written for a musical later performed by the Fisherfolk at the Edinburgh Festival Fringe) seemed to typify the spirit coming out of this new community movement: deep and gutsy and real. Sadly, Mikel Kennedy was killed in a car crash in 1998, but his songs are still sold on CD today.

But the song that really swept the UK when the Fisherfolk arrived was a children's song. Written by another young man at Redeemer, Brian Howard's *The Butterfly Song* was an instant hit, in demand at every ministry of the Fisherfolk. Part of it was probably because it was a very good song for children, with plenty of actions, but it also spoke directly to adults because of its message about self-acceptance (*If I were a butterfly, I'd thank you Lord for giving me wings......but I just thank you Father for making me 'me'*).

It was a fresh new sound that broke through the stuffiness of a lot of religious music at the time. But more importantly, the Fisherfolk incorporated it in adult services, thereby breaking another traditional pattern: the division between adults and children, with the implication that children's spirituality is trivial and unimportant while adult worship needs to be serious and reverential. Some of the more pompous religious personalities reacted testily, but most people loved it.

They also loved the unashamedly celebratory style of many of the songs, such as Ed Baggett's *We really want to thank you, Lord,* sung in a high energy, folk-rock style. This song stood in marked contrast to many worship songs of the time because it celebrated life in the here and now, speaking of *the gift of your body here on earth* and giving thanks *for our life together...tenderness which sets us free to serve you with our lives.* Few songs were so direct about the way God was experienced in real life. Most were meditations or worship of some attribute of God, or a prayer that God would transform human life in some way. Most people probably did feel that ordinary Christian life could do with a bit of input from God to make it more dynamic and uplifting, but here was a song that was speaking of actual current experience in church life.

Other songs would be sung as a round or as an "add on" where individuals could start a verse with their own variant of the original line. Again, the use of these songs in adult gatherings helped to break down barriers and encouraged congregational participation. They communicated a certain message, that the church was a body in which everyone belonged and worshiped as a body—they were not isolated individuals worshiping God in the privacy of their own souls. For example, a song such as *God has called you* by Diane Davis Andrew, where an individual's name would be inserted, would be a way of drawing people out of the isolation and anonymity of a large gathering.

Just as important as the songs themselves was the way they were sung and led. Worship was designed to be a corporate act. The function of leaders was to facilitate that, which meant avoiding techniques that gave it the feel of a performance. The arrangements of songs, the tempo, the strum of a guitar, even the type of guitar (usually a twelve string rather than a six string) all contributed to the sense of a united act of worship. Although the lead singers were disciplined vocally, in the Community everyone was taught how to sing, blending voices with others to produce the distinctive unified sound for which the Fisherfolk became well known. Provided worship was properly led, it was possible for an entire congregation to participate in it. The sound of the music was often thought to be a reflection of the relationships between the singers. In one sense it was true but the music was also inclusive. It drew others into it.

For me, singing was one of the biggest hurdles, more frightening than anything else about community life. I had grown up believing I was tone deaf and couldn't sing a note. One day Gary Miles, one of the Fisherfolk, got me in a room with a piano and had me sing to the notes he played. He persevered until I could approximate to the sounds, at which point he pronounced me a "low tenor." It was the first time anyone had ever attempted to define my singing voice, and it made an amazing difference to confidence in trying to blend with others. But it was taken for granted that everyone could and would be part of Community worship.

Betty Pulkingham was a prolific writer of songs and music, but she was probably most well known for her mass settings. Of these by far the most commonly used was the *Mass for the King of Glory*. This could be sung as a folk mass with just a guitar or with a full orchestra. Again, the way the various elements were played and sung was crucial to its effect. It transformed a routine service of communion into a complete act of worship.

The Church of England at that time was only just emerging from a Protestant heritage that elevated morning and evening prayer (with preaching of the word) as the primary focus of church life. Parish communion had been instituted as the main weekly service, but there was not a wide choice of music and the modern texts were still experimental. For many Anglicans (let alone Nonconformists) the word "Mass" meant a Catholic Mass or a high church ritual. Consequently the *King of Glory* Mass was their first exposure to a sung Eucharist. It put the Eucharist at the heart of this new "renewal" movement.

At the central point of the service, while people were filing up to take communion and for a while afterwards, the worship leadership group would play a number of songs in which the congregation would join, often spontaneously as it appeared (although spontaneity could be practiced—it was part of preparation for leading public worship).

This gave the feel of a service being "led by the Spirit." What many people were looking for in worship was a feeling of being in touch with the divine. Classic hymns and worship songs could achieve that effect, but often in an individualistic and even escapist kind of way, drawing the worshiper away from earth into heaven, so to speak. Community worship was rooted in the present (not least because those worshiping were encouraged to be aware of those around them rather than becoming "lost in wonder, love and praise"), yet the paradox was that it seemed to give people a transcendental experience that they rarely encountered in normal church life.

Fashions in music come and go, and it was inevitable that a folk idiom would eventually give way to other, more popular musical trends. Nevertheless, there were aspects of the Fisherfolk style of worship that remain important today.

One technique, for example, was to strip Victorian hymns of their four part harmonies so that they could be sung as a folk song with a variety of instruments and the organ. The point of this was not simply to give priority to "folk" as such, but to facilitate worship as a corporate act, using a tapestry of voices and instruments as a coherent whole.

Another reason was that songs tend to lose their reflective character when sung in parts. Without them they can tell a story. For the Community at least, this conveyed back to it a sense of its identity as a spiritual body of people, and those others who heard it and participated in it felt that they were sharing in that identity.

It made room for all, regardless of age or condition. A good deal of modern worship is extremely professional and competent, yet it appeals principally to the worshiper as an individual and to those who choose it by preference—in other words, it becomes a commodity rather than a true reflection of who the participants are.

Although a vast number of songs were in use, drawn from many different sources around the world, some of those written by Community members were directly related to the life. One such was Max Dyer's *'lu-ia, 'lu-ia*, which perfectly captured the spirit of the early days. Written not long before the move from Yeldall Manor to Cumbrae, the lyrics were a reflection of the willingness to go anywhere or do anything for God. *Feel a change a-comin', 'luia, 'luia, I will sing to you.* That was exactly the way it was. *Packed my bags today, 'luia, 'luia, Goin' far away, 'luia, 'luia, Whether I go or stay, 'luia, 'luia, I will sing to you.* This was the way everyone expected to relate to changes and moves: with a cheerful spirit.

Another of Max's songs, *Pullin' the weeds*, expressed what life was like at Yeldall Manor. The property had quite large grounds which were totally overgrown and required a major effort by teams of community members and visitors over many months to clear them. *Pullin' the weeds, Lord, pullin' the weeds, Livin' for your glory, pullin' the weeds* meant that whether you were a professional musician or a successful accountant or an internationally known celebrity, you were just as likely to find yourself cutting brambles on a damp English day — and that was fine, because that was the spirit of the time.

The measure of your worth and the joy of the Christian spirit did not depend on what you did. This was an add-on song, so others could add their own daily tasks such as *Sweepin' the floor, Lord*....

Some songs, such as Dave Porter's *There's a family gathering*, focused particularly on the nature of community life as a family, or as a body. Another example, very popular in ministry, was *The Celebration Song* by Jonathan Asprey and Tim Whipple. *For our life together, we celebrate*... often made a fitting end to an evening with the Fisherfolk or a weekend camp.

Not all songs were simple, or celebratory. Some were more like hymns, which addressed the darkness and pain of human life. Jodi Page-Clark's *Fear not, for I have redeemed you*, based on Isaiah 43, had a universal appeal because its language spoke to people's often inarticulate feelings about themselves and their need of God. Another of Jodi's songs, *Kyrie Eleison*, was a call to repentance, mission and commitment. It is interesting to compare some of the lines of *Kyrie Eleison* (*Forgive us, Father, hear our prayer/We would walk with you anywhere*) with those of the Victorian poet and hymn writer Frances Ridley Havergal (*Take my life and let it be/Consecrated, Lord to thee*). The latter hymn is essentially a personal dedication, whereas many of the Community songs were written in the first person plural, reflecting the Community's understanding of itself as the body of Christ. Jodi's songs had a particularly gutsy sound, combining theology with real feeling, which was reflected as much in the melody as in the words. In Fisherfolk ministry they could often get below people's skin during a time of worship.

The Fisherfolk also made extensive use of creative arts in worship: drama, dance, poetry and so on. Again, this was relatively unusual at the time, yet many a point could be made far more effectively by a simple sketch than by a sermon, and would often be much more memorable. Through community life and constant experience of ministry, many of the Fisherfolk developed into serious ministers. At the same time, there were many barriers to overcome. Although they were in great demand, there was also a certain stuffiness at big meetings that tended to relegate them to a "song and dance" act, preparatory to the main event which was an address by a big name speaker. It was a similar story in some churches, where they were expected to fill a worship "slot." However, the intention of the ministry was to show how an entire service could and should be a coherent act of worship by the body of believers as a whole. Worship, for the Community and the Fisherfolk, was never a slot.

One of the high water marks of Fisherfolk ministry at Cumbrae was the production of the musical for the Edinburgh Festival Fringe. It was inspired by the game of Monopoly. In the game, the family move around the board while the game master and referee Devv makes sure the rules are strictly kept. Of course, the rules guarantee that ultimately some get rich while others end up with nothing, but the family frustrate Devv by sharing all they have. It was a parable of community life and comment on the modern market economy. It was intended to show that economic life and relationships were at the heart of what it means to worship God.

Why was worship such a feature of community life? Graham Pulkingham always insisted that the Community were to be "a people of praise." The praise or worship of God is the basis of the spiritual energy that is released when people genuinely share their lives. By itself worship is like a cloud without rain if it merely rehearses spiritual or theological themes with little real connection to anything happening on the ground, however beautiful it may be. It does not automatically create commitment — that was a mistake made by many who thought they could achieve it by importing Fisherfolk-style worship. But without worship commitment becomes more like political theory or ideology through which people are controlled rather than inspired, energized and set free to be themselves.

Worship, that is, the instinct to idolize or adore, is of course a characteristic of all human beings. Secular worship is a familiar feature at public events held in large venues such as football stadiums. To worship is "to give worth to," which in turn means that it is always other centered. It can be corrupted, for example if the object of worship is inappropriate or the activity itself has more to do with satisfying certain needs or agendas than with a true act of worship, but in general worship is disinterested — it is not done for personal benefit. Hence Christian worship has two poles: on the one hand there is the "lost in wonder, love and praise" mode, while on the other there is the God-ward directed life, which can be extremely sacrificial. But these are not alternatives. They are part of a single orientation towards God, which for the Community meant both common life and the worship of lips that came out of that life.

Graham drew a distinction between public worship events, or the worship that took place on an outreach ministry, and the worship of the Community family. The former type was "prophetic" or "evangelistic," whereas the latter was an intensely pastoral event, even if it was a service to which guests or members of the public could be invited. Although the Community had its own specialists in liturgy, it was always felt important that everyone at least tried to understand what was happening.

To begin with, the Community were taught that each worship service was a unique event. It was a "now" thing; it could never be repeated at that time and place with exactly that group of people. This self evident fact was intended to inculcate the need to take it seriously. There had to be a fine sense of occasion, like a birthday party, which required planning, and it needed to appeal to the entire human being, through the use of all the ingredients of human communication. Even spontaneity, which was a kind of studied carelessness, could be planned and practiced. It was a family affair. People often use worship to meet their own needs, for example by being over-enthusiastic, but here the event needed to be appropriate in the sense that it expressed "who we are at this point in time."

To make it happen, it needed people with the gift of bringing the senses alive.

Graham hated rubrics. They were fine as printed instructions in an order of service, but they should play no part in spoken worship. There should be no verbal instructions such as "let us pray" or "now we shall sing hymn number such and such." There should be no "clergy voice." These kinds of things lacked the sense of family and gave a service more of a feel of a stage performance. They felt like something imposed, or even a crutch designed to produce an atmosphere of reverence through artificial means.

A worship service had to be understood as an event in which God was gathering his people together for a purpose. This was not a mere pious thought, but expressed the nature of worship itself. Corporate worship was reflective; it was not a mere activity. It was in a sense a dialogue with God. According to Graham, in many churches people were bored with church; they wanted to get the service over and done with as soon as possible so that they could get on with their lives.

There was little sense of hearing God or dialogue with God. Charismatic worship was often characterized by a fear of silence, betraying an unreflective spirit. People felt they had to be singing praises or praying all the time. In contrast, reflective worship was a creative introspection about God or about what God was saying.

The treasury of scripture is rich with prose and poetry, symbolism and metaphor, which tell of the great themes of health, life and salvation. In Graham's words, these needed to "sing deep within our souls" and the way that could happen was through reflection. Many people thought reflection was something done in silence and in private, but in corporate life it was neither necessarily. For example the Psalter was an entire book of reflection, though it took a disciplined congregation to sing psalms effectively. The general point was that scripture provided a sense of heritage, a family history so to speak, and worship services needed to be structured around what God was saying to his people.

In Graham's view, corporate worship primarily involved listening and speaking. It did not exclude private, internal worship, but it was not the main place for that. It was not a "vertical" communication that took place within the soul. It required at least two people, who heard God and spoke to God through normal means of human communication. Even the gifts of the Spirit were exercised as "horizontal" communication: something heard, spoken and able to be judged objectively.

Hence the idea of corporate worship as a mere multiplicity of individual communications with God was always resisted in community life. For example, the notion of peace was not understood to mean peace of mind or peace with God in an individualistic sense. Nor did it mean absence of conflict, but victory over conflict. It was a communal word, a gift from God that was never perfectly attained in this age. Thus, to greet one another with the peace *in worship* was to say something about community relationships: to acknowledge the conflicts in community life but to celebrate the victory being accomplished over them. That was at the heart of all community worship. Liturgically the custom was to hug rather than give a handshake or a kiss. That was unusual in those days, but it helped establish the physical, concrete nature of worship, breaking down the barriers both between men and women and between men and men.

The choice of songs obviously depended on the occasion, but in general the Community avoided excessive emphasis on themes and tried to achieve a balance between traditional hymnody and modern songs. Traditional hymns are not just yesterday's music. They are the songs that have survived, out of many written over centuries, because of their timeless quality. Most modern songs will be forgotten a hundred years from now, but some may survive if they find acceptance beyond a certain constituency. Many popular songs today express a theology that is limited, even if appealing to a large number. Typically, the focus is on devotion to Jesus, with music to match. True worship is seen as an outpouring of the heart to God. Yet the Community rarely found subjective worship of God helpful in supporting its life. It always seemed too private, too detached from the real world in which Christ lives today.

For example, in renewal movements, a common feature of worship is the repetition of words such as "glory" or "hallelujah," expressions that are repeated as if their meaning is self-evident, though if you were to ask someone what exactly the word "glory" refers to, you might get a rather vague or confused answer. Such words are frequently used as general expressions of praise and worship. In community life, though, it was always understood that the glory of God is reflected in lives, not in words and phrases.

Glory is the earthy presence of God. Graham once said that he was more "glorious" than another Community member simply because he had more bulk!

Glory is not some sort of Shekinah light, a product of the religious imagination. Rather, it is something tangible or palpable, which evokes praise and admiration. So in community, the worship event was a summation of their experience of God's glory in everyday life. Since God is present in both the good and the bad, all of it was brought into Community worship so that, in principle at least, it could be seen — otherwise the glory of God would have been lost. Some think pain means God is absent. It seems unnatural to give thanks in the midst of suffering. But God is in all of it, and hence Community worship celebrated both the incarnation of God in Jesus Christ and God's redeeming presence in a world full of pain. Liturgy — the "work of the people" — was the principal vehicle for this. This outlook highlighted several aspects of corporate worship, both negative and positive. Problems included routine, simply repeating a formula that has worked in the past; the assumption that content matters more than method (it doesn't matter how you sing a song; just as long as something fitting is chosen); piety (excessively devotional language, or the imposition of theological agendas); the cult of personality, focusing so much attention on what is happening up front that the event becomes like spiritual entertainment. On the positive side, details and mechanics of worship were taken seriously, discipline and the commitment to practice were taken for granted and planning was thorough.

Although in principle anyone was welcome to a Community Eucharist, corporate worship was always seen as an intentional act by the group as a whole. It was not a public event, staged by a small team, to which people simply turned up.

What the Community were trying to achieve in their worship was a sense both of the unity of the Body and of its inclusiveness. Neither the performance oriented approach nor the attitude of "this is the way we do things here" were likely to succeed in that. The word "inclusive" today tends to have political overtones, but in that environment it simply meant that everyone had a place and worship needed to reflect that reality. Community members were a disparate bunch consisting of men, women and children of different nationalities, churches and theological viewpoints. To make room for all of them did not mean catering for people's tastes; it meant a form of worship that allowed them to be who they were without feeling as if they did not belong.

Choosing a church because it suits reduces Christian faith to the level of a commodity, locking its leaders in to the pursuit of relevance and throwing up leaders who are skilled in tuning in to people's feelings and needs. Of course this may be inevitable, but worship itself then becomes a commodity, peddled through the media or commercial stores like any other form of music. Here, it becomes detached from its true purpose, losing its essential connection to the visible, palpable body of Christ. It becomes exclusive, and no matter how much the church might proclaim that "all are welcome," it is clear that only those who fit in will be comfortable. Worship in the Community of Celebration always tried to give a different message.

Chapter 11

Relationships

Once, on a visit to Post Green, a Baptist minister was invited to supper at one of the households. After the meal he declared that he disagreed with community living, on the ground that it caused people to sin where there would otherwise be none. His hosts were too polite to take issue with him, but found the statement almost unbelievable coming from such a source.

Whatever was meant by the word "sin," it was surely obvious that such behavior was not caused by others but arose from issues already existing within a person's own spiritual and psychological make up—for which they needed to take full responsibility. If avoiding "sin" was the touchstone of godliness, it would not only limit the ability of Christians to work together but would also soon degenerate into hypocrisy.

And perhaps that was the problem with church life. The effort to live by a supposedly higher standard than that of "the world" led to a manner of life and relating that was unreal—and, at worst, dishonest. Despite claims that Christians are "sinners saved by grace," the impression given to outsiders (and even to those within the church) was that Christians were either hypocrites pretending to be saints or else too good to join. If the standard was impeccable behavior, that was too big a barrier for most people.

Yet behavior was important. Words like "sin" implied that behavior was a matter of obeying God's laws (with all the potential that has for lip service and denying the facts of one's own humanity), but Graham Pulkingham preferred to put it another way. "If you are not here to love," he would say, "this is not the place for you."

Love makes room for the other's faults, but just as important, it makes room for one's own. To love does not make you inhuman; it makes you vulnerable, and in so doing it makes you more human.

Thus, in community people were not Christians pretending to be good; they were people trying to love one another without denying the truth of their own humanity. This made them extremely vulnerable to each other, and it was true that in some cases the pain of it was too much to bear. Withdrawal was the only option. For a few, that could mean leaving the Community. For others, particularly where a household situation looked as if it was stuck in an unhealthy dynamic, it might mean moving to another household. More generally it could mean a kind of emotional withdrawal, which was instantly felt by the other person. Consequently people were encouraged, by teaching and pastoral counsel, to stay open and to work through the difficulties.

In the early days in Britain, people had to be taught very simple things that might sound obvious, such as not using accusatory language like "you always" or "you never." Apart from the fact that such statements could rarely be substantiated, they carried an emotional weight that would only be felt as an attack, and therefore likely to put the other person on the defense. The fact that another person made you angry did not mean that they had done something wrong, or that you had been injured in some way. Others, confronted by the same behavior, did not get angry. First and foremost the task was to acknowledge the response you were having yourself, which was your responsibility and which, in all likelihood, had little to do with what the other person said or did.

For example, one young woman was driven to rage by the way one of the men drove a car. (It so happened that the car was his, but was being used in the community car pool.) "He is *so controlling,*" she said intensely. "The way he sits there, with his hand on the wheel. I can't stand it." The man concerned was a person with deep seated problems requiring medical treatment, and had a big issue with anger. What the young woman was picking up was probably accurate; body language is often as eloquent as words. More to the point, however, was her response. She had no room within herself for that kind of behavior. Without examining her own reactions, what she brought to the situation could have been any number of things, from attitudes to men in general to cultural difference.

Of course, it might well be that the original cause of offense was in fact inappropriate or even damaging in some way. The possibilities in community life were endless, from "bad mouthing" to neglect or careless use of property, from an occasional flashpoint to a habitual way of relating.

Cultural differences were a prolific source of tension. The classic example of squeezing a tube of toothpaste at the end or in the middle will have to stand for myriads of instances where habits or a certain outlook were the cause of a relationship spat. Sometimes there were genuine disagreements about the importance of hygiene or tidiness. But in all these cases, the onus was on you to "own" where you were coming from and not to dump it on the other person as if they were at fault. If they *were* at fault, it was up to you to say what had hurt you without accusatory overload, and if that was too difficult you might need a third person to help create the space. The golden rule was to stay open, so that at the end of a difficult conversation you always parted with a hug.

The official jargon for an emotional confrontation was "vigorous fellowship." If that sounds antiseptic, it also reflects the fact that Christians cannot avoid altercations on occasions.

Some of those coming into community life had been taught, implicitly if not explicitly, that this was wrong: Christians should always be loving and not give way to their anger. But suppressing or denying emotions does not resolve relationship issues; it is more likely to stoke resentment that comes out with greater force on a later occasion, probably in an inappropriate way. It also tends to reinforce the perception of right and wrong. Hence Community members were always taught that it was more important to love than to be right, provided they were not in denial about their own feelings and emotions.

My recollections of "relationship" incidents in early years include many flashback memories, of people glaring at each other across a table, throwing jugs of water or milk at each other, jumping out of a window and running away, pinning someone up against a wall, punching a hole in a door. It all added a bit of spice to life, and was accepted without judgment as something that happened from time to time. But in the vast majority of cases, relationship issues were resolved peaceably by taking the time to talk.

With families, there were often some tight, difficult dynamics that were not easy to break into. Patterns of relating had become entrenched and routine. They involved both adults and children. Hence, particularly in the early days, the Community was willing to place families in larger households that might include other families. This would not happen without pastoral support, but it often had the effect of breaking up family dynamics and even precipitating pastoral issues where one family's "ethos" predominated over the other. Generally the longevity of a household in these circumstances was not too long; just enough to open up the dynamics and address what was really going on.

However, one of the most effective ways of dealing with family dynamics was through the life itself, in which every person was treated as an individual in their own right. This enabled people to pursue interests, make friendships and generally grow and develop as individuals apart from their partners.

The nuclear family as a building block of society suffers from the problem that no single individual can fully meet the needs of another, mentally, emotionally and spiritually. In less individualistic societies there is always the possibility of wider networks that help give a person a sense of their identity. Thus in the Community men did not always have to be in traditional male roles, nor were women confined to housewife roles. This created space and often took pressure off the marriage dynamics.

Nevertheless, what was intended as a benefit did sometimes produce unexpected results. Typically, a wife might suddenly discover there was more to life than being at home doing cooking and cleaning, and would quite like the freedom to grow in other ways. A former housewife might turn out to be an excellent administrator or a good counselor or a talented musician. Occasionally, when this happened, the husband might have a crisis of identity. For men, work is often as much about identity as it is about fulfillment, so these outcomes provided an opportunity to work with individuals on issues of identity—which were often at the heart of marriage dynamics, though difficult to isolate in the context of nuclear family life.

It is one thing to tell a person that their identity is in Christ as someone beloved of God, but it is quite another matter to get them to believe it. For many, both men and women, job or role was crucial in giving them a sense of their identity and worth. In society at large in the sixties and seventies, including the church, marriage was often a key source of identity, especially for women. It was one of the factors that made marriage a desirable goal and put pressure on marriages that already existed. It also had damaging effects on those who were, for whatever reason, unmarried. It made them feel like second class citizens, and they may well have been treated as such.

Hence one of the most important functions of community life was to give people a new sense of their identity. In this kind of milieu, theological words were not concepts that just had to be believed; they were a descriptive language helping people to put words to what they were experiencing.

The Community ethos was to treat every individual with dignity and respect, no matter who they were, and there is no question that this was a potent remedy for a misplaced sense of identity. It also had an interesting effect in that it seemed to reduce the heavy pressure of secular society to achieve fulfillment by getting married. Of course, people did marry in community, but what was noticeable was the lack of preoccupation with it.

Another related issue was gender relationships.

The priority of love meant that the Community tended to take a pragmatic attitude to this rather than either a theological or a political/ideological position. For example, there was then (as there is now) a section of the church that believed in the subordination of women, on the basis of pastoral advice given by the Apostle Paul to some of his first century churches.

This made little sense in community life. "Love" was not a doctrinaire concept; it was something self evident, felt and experienced in common humanity. In community you had to be real and give people their dignity as persons—whoever they were. On the other hand, although some members did have strong opinions on the subject, the Community was not as strongly ideological as some other communities. It tended to move with the times. Thus, at the Church of the Redeemer in the sixties there were no women on the body of elders, but by the time that system was abandoned by the Community of Celebration they had been included for some time.

As years went by households tended to get smaller and moves less frequent. The largest had been 25 people or more, but eventually the average came down to around seven or eight. It was also less common to put two families together. Many people had lived in community for a long time, and hence some of the old pastoral techniques fell by the wayside. What replaced them were the emerging techniques of self analysis and self examination.

Why was it, for example, that a person habitually found another individual difficult? Why did some people constantly feel left out, ignored or worthless, and why was it that some scenarios seemed to repeat themselves endlessly, like a broken record?

The Community's association with Frank Lake began out of a mutual interest in these kinds of issues. The techniques generally referred to as "rebirthing" were a new thing in those days, and quite controversial. Frank had developed what was known as Primal Therapy. His original experiments with LSD had given way to a deep breathing technique that enabled a client to recover memories as far back as birth or even earlier. But he recognized that this kind of procedure often left the subject feeling extremely exposed and vulnerable. He saw the Community as an ideal environment where support would be at hand. He also wanted to integrate the therapy into a theological and spiritual framework.

Many Community members from Cumbrae and Post Green did the therapy, some of them several times. It was a useful tool for a while. Many came to a better understanding of themselves, which, in itself, was an important step in personal growth or healing. But it was not the same thing as a cure. The law of diminishing returns meant that repeating the therapy did not improve results significantly, and how much difference it made long term for the average person is debatable. As with all therapy and counseling, information and expression of feeling can only take a person so far. Then there comes a point at which it is necessary to work with what has been achieved. For Christians, this generally crosses over into the spiritual arena.

Psychological damage, like physical damage, often cannot be cured; it takes spirit to overcome it or rise above it. Consequently the Community always tried to link psychological technique with spiritual exercises and with prayer and worship.

There were other techniques, such as the Myers Briggs analytical system or the more esoteric Enneagram. They could be helpful, but again it depended on how they were used. Working with the results was one thing, but they could be used to categorize people. Comments such as "I'm a T" or "That's because you're a J" (as if that excused or explained everything) did not help personal growth or community life. There was always the risk that such pursuits could become almost addictive, as if personal growth was the main purpose of life.

Nevertheless, the interest in these techniques, although fueled to some extent by their novelty at the time, did reflect a genuine concern in the Community. Recognizing the effects of long term involvement in community life later led to calls for psychological testing of new members to determine their suitability. Some other communities, including religious orders, already did this.

Several Community members with no formal training in counseling or therapy acquired a high degree of skill in both, later going on to gain a professional qualification. This was another example of how community life could be empowering, with the needs of ministry calling out gifts to produce a solution that was creative for everyone concerned.

Many people have commented about the uniqueness of relationships in the Community of Celebration. Actually, the word "relationships" is slightly misleading. It often carries the sense of interpersonal relationships, which is certainly one aspect of the subject. But for many who belonged to the Community over the years, there is a different meaning: a sense of relationship with people whom they scarcely know.

In some ways, one analogy might be that of veterans of a war. People who lived in the Community, especially in the earlier years, were a bit like soldiers in battle: disciplined, prepared to rough it in any situation, ready to move when required, battle scarred from various bruising encounters but also sharing the deep comradeship of commitment to one another. It is not a bad analogy but it is not the whole story. What people experienced, in tough times and smooth, was a kind of friendship that recognized and affirmed who they were.

The basis of this was common life, where everything was shared and commitment to one another was wholehearted. This meant that everyone coming into the Community was received in the same way. A local tradesman was as likely to find congenial company as the most religious of visitors. Although the nitty-gritty of everyday life might test such friendship to the limits, requiring a high level of mutual commitment to work through the problems, it did not depend on the intensity of personal relationships for its existence. It was actually the Community spirit, which treated all human beings as if they were, in the Apostle Paul's words, "members one of another," people of dignity and worth.

In normal life, many things militate against this way of relating. Large areas of life are kept private, as far as possible, from money to personal habits and foibles. There is a subtle (or not so subtle) pressure to compete, to present oneself in the best light possible. There are all kinds of criteria (color, gender, education and so on) that are used to grade people, consciously or unconsciously, on some sort of scale of acceptance or worth. The church is by no means immune from this; in fact, in church there are other factors such as theological correctness or religious enthusiasm to add to the mix. All these factors cause people to try to conform, in order to gain acceptance.

It is quite rare to find acceptance at a deeply human level that is not based on any of these things. Hence relationships in the Community, in this broad sense, were experienced as something special, linking people for decades after they had left, including even some who left in anger. Conversely, some of those who moved on subsequently found it difficult to integrate back into church life.

For the Community, pastoral and therapeutic techniques were tools to help overcome some of the difficulties encountered in community life. They were not a cure-all, nor were they an end in themselves. Their use depended on circumstances and the availability of gifts. The one constant was worship, in which all manner of things could be offered to God. It was not uncommon, in community worship, to see someone with tears running down their face. This was where the spiritual dimension of community relationships found its source and its energy. Here, common human life with its murky compromises and its pain was no longer banal. In some mysterious way it became invested with the divine.

Chapter 12

The "Son of God" teachings

Graham Pulkingham was primarily a pastor. He had little time for abstract theological principles and was much more concerned about working with people in their spiritual problems. His talks were not without preparation but he would speak at length without notes, frequently engaging with his audience by inviting responses or questions. There was little obvious structure to his addresses. He would go round and round the subject, often going off at a tangent or speaking very quickly and incisively to ram home a point. It made it quite difficult to take notes or to distil the essence of what he was saying.

Nevertheless, people got the message because he was speaking to where they were. There was often laughter in Graham's talks because he would always puncture the absurdities and pomposities of church life. He would also address real problems, which were often ignored in conventional preaching or skated over with platitudes and religious panaceas.

At the same time he was uncompromising in his language. On the one hand he held out a vision which made people feel they were being confronted with some sort of ideal that could never be attained in this life, even if it was what they believed. On the other hand he was almost brutal in the way he exposed the petty compromises and evasions that people use to avoid facing up to their beliefs. He was always trying to narrow the gap between belief and reality. One thing could always be said about Graham: he got people's attention.

In Graham's mind, at the core of Christian faith was the question of identity. People had beliefs, which they might well adhere to tenaciously, but in real life they struggled. For some, belief slowly withered. Others maintained some semblance of Christian life and behavior but were also unsure, afraid and protective of their own lives and interests. For Graham, this came down to a defective sense of identity.

One of his core teachings was the "son of God" message (Romans 8.14: "all that are led by the Spirit of God are sons of God"). For Graham this defined Christian identity. As this was in the days before the introduction of inclusive language, he was able to use the term "son" to draw out the particular nuance attaching to that word, i.e. not gender but identity with, and inheritance of characteristics from, the father.

Starting with belief in God as Father, Son and Holy Spirit, belief in the Son meant that you identified yourself with Jesus who took all human sin into the grave and rose to new life. That meant you no longer needed to live under condemnation. To believe in the *Spirit* was to believe that, as a result of what Jesus did, the Holy Spirit was now available with power for those who believed in him to overcome the works of darkness. So if you "receive the Spirit" only as some sort of personal blessing, in Graham's words "you make Jesus a liar" (the brutal language, calculated to make people sit up and take notice). To believe in the Holy Spirit in the true sense, you had to *both* accept it as a gift *and* go and live as Jesus did.

One of Graham's favorite analogies was the story of Abraham. In the story of Abraham God tells him to leave his country and kinsmen and go to an unknown country. He takes his nephew Lot, but it is not until he is separated from Lot that God starts to do what he intended, which was to raise up offspring by

Abraham through which the whole world would be blessed. He is 75 years old when he first hears God's call and leaves his home. He doesn't agonize over it or try to test God. He just accepts it, and because of that he was called the father of the faithful.

In modern spiritual life, according to Graham, we have no problem listening to God or hearing God, but we do have a big problem trusting ourselves. So in Abraham's position (75 years old, hearing a call to leave home) *our* response would be, "Am I really hearing God or is it just me?" This, said Graham, showed a lack of faith in Jesus, because what he had achieved made anyone who believed in him also a son of God. "Son of God" was not a title, nor did it have anything to do with gender or status. It was about who you were. A "son of God" (unlike many modern day Christians) would have no difficulty recognizing God speaking and trusting it.

If you were the son of the British monarch, for example, you knew who you were and so did everyone else. You didn't have to do anything to prove it. You had a self conscious knowledge. But it was by no means common for Christians to have such an awareness of themselves as sons of God. Many Christians preferred to describe themselves as "sinners saved by grace." Graham disliked that phrase, which was self deprecatory even if true.

The word "sinner" was a description of who you were, not what you did. Jesus was not a sinner; he was the Son of God, so if his life was in you then the life you now lived was God's life. And for Graham there was no separation between God's life and any other form of life. The "Spirit" was not an alien force residing within you. It was not a kind of therapeutic intervention that worked with varying degrees of success in curing the maladies of the soul. The life you lived in your full humanity was either God's life or it wasn't. If you were not a son of God you did not belong to God at all: if you were, you should be conscious of it all the time. You needed to stand up.

In practice, however, many Christians confronted with this theology had an embarrassed response, even though they might read and sing about it. That was because they had not accepted it; it was not their self image. But for Graham you could not separate your life from God's life that easily. "If God withdrew his life from you, you would literally fall down dead," he would say. That was a typical piece of hyperbole to show that you could not divide yourself from God with the kind of dualistic thinking characteristic of western Christians, whereby spiritual life and natural life are imagined as two separate kinds of existence.

But what about the real problems? Graham himself was often in conversation with people who said "I believed that once, a long time ago, but it didn't work out so I've grown cold or I've modified my position."

What was needed, Graham said, was constant encouragement to be awakened to our beliefs. In the story Abraham was 75 years old before he heard God's call and had to wait another 25 years before receiving the promise in the shape of his son Isaac. The story tells us he simply accepted the fact that he would have a son and heir, even though he was too old.

Hence Abraham became "father of the faithful" in two respects. First, he heard God and believed that it was God, not his own imagination, and second, he was a faithful man, i.e. he had integrity. He was not fearful and had no self rejection. The problem for many people was not that God did not speak to them but that they did not know what to do with it — they were wishy-washy. They were trying to be a son of God by imitating the jargon or reading the right books, but they never seemed to be able to make it. That was because "son of God" was an order of being, not something you did. "You can't become a dog by barking," Graham would say. Either you were a son of God or you weren't. If you were, that was your identity.

So Graham was always encouraging Community members, when they got up in the morning, to look at themselves in the mirror and say "Good morning, son of God." A life of peace meant walking in that conscious awareness. It was a habit of mind that in his view would lead to a remarkable transformation of life. And when people with that self awareness came together, there could be an extraordinary release of power for living.

Another related teaching was that of the elder-younger relationship. Again, Graham related to this from a pastoral point of view, not as a doctrine.

In the ancient world of Jesus, it was normal practice for the eldest son to inherit the bulk of the estate. The father was the head of the clan, who effectively owned everything, made decisions and provided for all those in his care. The eldest son was trained up to take over that position—a practice common even in Britain amongst the landowning classes. In the process he would learn all about the father's responsibilities, how he made decisions and what the ethos of the family was.

It seems that Jesus used this model to describe his relationship to God. For example, he called God "Father" and referred to himself as "the Son." He talked about sharing everything with the Father and doing his will. This comes out particularly in the Gospel of John. "The Son can do nothing of himself, except what he sees his Father doing; for whatever the Father does, that the Son does likewise. For the Father loves the Son and shows him everything that he himself is doing" (5.19-20). The picture here is of the eldest son absorbing all that it means to be the same person as his father, ultimately taking over the reins of the clan.

Jesus used the same model in the parable of the Prodigal Son. In this story the eldest son complains that his father has never given him anything to enjoy with his friends. The father responds by saying "You are my son. Everything I have is yours." The eldest son has come of age and has entered into his inheritance even though the father is still alive. The two are supposed to be as one.

Graham saw this as a means by which spiritual truths are communicated. In time Jesus became effectively a father to his own disciples, who in turn passed on the "family ethos" to their disciples. What was passed on was not just theological doctrine but a spirit, a way of being that permeated the church.

In particular, Graham saw this as the means by which the spirit of the Community of Celebration was passed on. The mechanics of living in community were straightforward enough, and in many respects common to many other communities. What was much less common was the spirit of the life, which was hard to put into words or at least hard to describe in a systematic way. It had to be felt and experienced rather than described. It was a collective spirit in which everyone felt they received unconditional acceptance, dignity and respect. It was a spirit of celebration through which joy and pain could both be offered to God and sanctified in the process. Through the sharing and celebration of common life together, at some level everyone felt they had been touched by the divine. This was not something that could be taught in a classroom.

Graham may have been over-optimistic in thinking that a whole community could learn this by being in some form of "elder-younger" relationship. Generally, relationships in the Community were at a peer level, even if (in the early years) some were designated as pastors. The latter tended to be authority figures rather than ministers drawing a younger person into relationship with them. Thus the "elder-younger" teaching did not generally continue beyond the early days at Yeldall Manor. However, Graham himself did continue to relate to his own vision in that way.

It was common in the Community for people to travel in pairs. Graham frequently travelled with Bill Farra, one of the original ministers who came to Britain from Houston. But Bill was more than just a traveling companion. He attended most of the formative meetings that shaped community life and in course of time emerged as the primary leader of the Community. Because of his relationship with Graham, he was one of the few who felt confident in challenging him. Graham for his part trusted Bill because he felt that his own vision was safe with him. This was an example of the "elder-younger" relationship working out in Graham's ministry, even if it was never described as such.

Fundamental to the "son of God" teachings was the desire to address Christian life at a spiritual level. That may sound strange—after all, it is presumably what every minister is supposed to be doing every week in every church—but in fact spirituality is often fairly low on the church agenda. Other concerns predominate, notably the problems of dealing with congregations whose commitment and capacity are limited. Often there are religious and theological agendas that control even the ministers themselves. It is rare to be able to work with a whole group of people at a spiritual level, and rarer still to work with a group that contains families.

Normally, individuals pursue their own spiritual journey to the extent that they will or can. Some get to grips with Christian spirituality in an intentional way through the monastic life—a life which incidentally involves community living, as a rule. In the Community of Celebration, real spiritual issues were being addressed among people who had never taken vows and in most cases never intended to. The average community member, if there was such a thing, was indistinguishable from the average member of a church congregation. They included families with children, who were subject to all the compromises and contingencies that limit what is possible in terms of commitment.

But that was the genius of the Community. It provided a way for ordinary people, the kind who would never become professional ministers or vowed monastics, to live the type of dedicated Christian life that would normally only be expected of people who had a special vocation. Not only that, but it made such a life homely and everyday, a life that anyone could join in even if they had little in the way of Christian faith. In principle, it was the kind of life that could and should be reflected in every church. But it did require, at the heart of it, the capacity to confront spiritual issues head on rather than simply accept the restrictions imposed by culture and tradition.

To stand a chance of reproducing the extraordinary years at the Church of the Redeemer, and to lay a solid foundation for the vision of a future religious order, there had to be the kind of teaching that would transform people's imagination and make it possible to pass the secret on. Graham never went into print with his ideas, probably because his position was always provi-sional—he was always working with people to give them the tools they needed to deal with their current situation. The "son of God" teachings did not outlast the first few years of the Community of Celebration, but they remain in its corporate memory through the recollection of all that happened in those formative years.

Chapter 13

Religious and secular life

From its earliest beginnings, the Community of Celebration was a religious community. It was not monastic, but it had the basic features of such communities, that is, it had its own sacramental life and was subject to the authority of the Anglican diocese in which it was situated. It did not fulfill the usual range of offices, but it did have Bible sharing in the morning, family worship in the evening and a regular weekly Eucharist. These later developed into the modified form of offices that exists today.

One might imagine that this would generate a highly charged religious atmosphere in comparison to normal church life, where most corporate activity is concentrated into a single day. Certainly there was a lot of religious activity, yet it did not feel the same as the churches people were used to. In some indefinable way, it seemed more natural and less intense. This was probably something to do with the relationship between religious and secular life in community.

One working definition of religion might be "taking God seriously." We come to God for a variety of reasons or motives, but once the connection is made we are continually faced with the choice of how far or how seriously we want to take it. This project is the purpose of religion.

Religion has two aspects, concerning God and the self. Any encounter with God draws us into worship. There is an imperative to this, not in the sense of a rule to be obeyed, but in the sense that human beings are worshiping creatures. This is not something accepted intellectually; it comes from within. But as we open ourselves to God, we also discover a major challenge to our humanity. We are liable to employ all manner of rationalizations and evasions to avoid facing up to the challenge. Taking God seriously therefore goes hand in hand with being serious about oneself and one's own life.

This was how Community members thought about it; they were being real about their religious beliefs and the implications. People used to talk about not being "Sunday" Christians. Yet at the same time the very process of taking beliefs seriously seemed to generate a conflict with conventional religion, even of the most devoted kind. It depended to some extent on the individual and the particular background from which they came.

My own background made me acutely aware of religious expectations and demands. To be a Christian involved adherence to a variety of beliefs and practices, often specific to a certain church or spiritual tradition. Although nobody claimed that theirs was the one true faith, in practice the social pressure (reinforced by teaching and preaching) made you feel that failure to conform to expected norms was in some way deviant from God's will. In community, on the other hand, being serious about God meant you had to be open to people whose spiritual life had been formed in a different tradition. They were as serious as you were, so you had no option but to try to keep to what was really important in Christian faith, even if it challenged previously held assumptions and religious custom.

Broadly speaking the major religions of the world convey their truths through mythology or stories of the gods. This means their deepest truths are communicated through stories and metaphors rather than explicit teaching. But in Christianity at least, there is often a tendency to relate to heavenly beings almost as if they are characters on a stage, rather than trying to get to grips with what they represent. Thus Jesus is an object of worship, for example, but the idea of reproducing "Jesus" in the modern world may be considered eccentric. The idea that "Jesus is Lord" has greater appeal, because it allows people to claim the benefits of allegiance to Jesus whilst at the same time being able to blend into the secular culture without too much difficulty.

Hence the Community was never comfortable with slogans such as "Jesus is Lord," although the situation was not as polarized as that statement makes it sound. By focusing on the realization of Jesus' sayings in real life, the problems of religious life were exposed because Jesus himself was frequently in conflict with religion, especially its dogmatic character, which creates a legal atmosphere with a body of expert opinion. Dogma has the inflexible character of law, which in practice applies also to inferences from dogma. A religious milieu is therefore often characterized by laws, certainties and judgments. It tends to spawn religious groups defining themselves by their submission to God's laws.

But in real life there are many gaps, and Jesus frequently occupied them. He challenged the practice of inferences-made-into-laws ("you have heard it said...but I say"), and dismissed the credentials of religious experts ("woe to you scribes..."). He confronted the religious spirit, supposedly careful in its obedience to God, by showing that in many cases it was directly *opposed* to the will of God. He was accused of being antinomian, rejecting the obligation to obey God's law, but his real battle was against control and exclusion on the basis of religious criteria. In his ministry life was not tidy and people did not fit the pattern. To "love God and your neighbor as yourself" was a principle that could potentially undermine virtually every religious law there was.

It was this model, rather than the model of a religious group in radical obedience to God's law, that inspired the Community. That did not make it easy. The sayings of Jesus could demand everything, even life itself, from those who followed them. But it was the spirit of them that was important. It was this that often felt ill at ease with enthusiastic devotion to Jesus as "Lord."

Spiritual insight does not derive from acceptance of dogma, yet it is the defense of dogma that preoccupies the religious spirit. For example the spiritual truth of the resurrection is lost when it is defended simply as an exciting historical event. Using a bit of hyperbole, we might say that anyone who is afraid of death doesn't believe in the resurrection. If we include in that the use of all the institutions in society that bolster us against the prospect of death and loss, that probably includes most people, including the stoutest believers in the resurrection.

Yet there is nothing like questioning its historicity for generating white heat in religious debate. The fact that most of us live as if the resurrection never happened, and believe in it as if it had no immediate practical consequence, is irrelevant. In fact, to live the truth of the resurrection fully in any concrete way might well be resisted on the grounds that, if not actually unscriptural, it is at most a specialist calling for a few.

Thus Christians themselves are not immune from confrontation with the Spirit of Jesus. Wherever Christian faith is understood in terms of rituals, beliefs, propositions, rules of various kinds, accepted practices, appropriate language, membership of an institution, codes of behavior and so on, it is likely to meet this collision, even if a belief seems plainly stated in scripture or hallowed by long tradition. Often, in his own life, Jesus appeared to set aside what were universally believed to be God's laws, and he had no hesitation in restating established beliefs. Using Paul's imagery, we might say it's called growing up.

A passage in Ephesians (4.14-16) expresses this particularly well. Paul urges his converts to "no longer be children, tossed by the waves and carried around by every wind of teaching." Some see in this a warning to avoid weird and wonderful beliefs, but the biggest reason why people are "tossed by the waves" is because beliefs are touted as normative for all Christians. They do not have to be weird or heretical; they may very well be widely accepted ideas within "normal" Christianity. There are plenty of "winds of teaching" in the church today, and often it is the conservative ones that have the greatest ability to toss to and fro. They can induce feelings of uncertainty, making those not thoroughly at home in their faith feel that they should be doing this or not doing that. In the case of the Galatians, Paul says they have been "bewitched" by what they have taken on board. That is the power of the religious imperative. To overcome it, according to Paul, we need to grow up, to quit being children. In other words, we need to behave like Jesus did.

The metaphor here is not just physical and emotional maturity but spiritual maturity. There are many broad issues in religion that call for this: the political use of religion; the use of religion as a means of comfort; the question of other religions and whether there is only one way to God; the relationship of historical to religious truth, or of dogma to real human life; to name but a few. Often these issues are basically decided by expediency or a feel-good factor or a legalistic approach, rather than in the authentic Spirit of Jesus. In every generation there is a need to re-establish a connection to the authentic Jesus, for spiritual vigor comes from him and the realization of his sayings, not from religious enthusiasm or political commitment.

What Jesus represents is the unity of divinity and humanity. This is frequently insisted upon or proclaimed as a dogma, but what it really does is act as a corrective to the human imagination of what God is like. For example, many people have a preferred image of God, such as a lawgiver or a lover. The one can lead to a moralistic outlook while the other may result in the kind of tolerance that demands nothing of anyone. Jesus, it has to be said, seems to have spent most of his time combating the first outcome, but there is no doubt that his vision demanded everything of those who followed him. Jesus' Spirit puts all our concepts of God into their proper perspective.

Thus his *allegorical* teaching ("the kingdom of God is like...") showed that mystical truth is allusive rather than definitive, allowing plenty of room to maneuver. On the other hand, his *direct* teaching (for example, "don't be anxious about tomorrow") challenged his hearers to trust and embrace God in a way that few dare contemplate.

The actual word "religion" is hardly mentioned at all in the Bible. One reference in James says that true religion is "to visit orphans and widows in their oppression, and to keep oneself without stain from the world" (1.27). Widows and orphans were a symbol of the weak and helpless in oppression—of whom there were a great many in those days. They were the ones who were closest to God's heart; in fact, Jesus identified himself with them. Reaching out to these "little ones", bringing them comfort and defending their cause, is, remarks James, the first priority of religion. It reflects Jesus' own teaching about the "little ones", which said that that was where he was to be found, if anyone was interested in serving him: in other words, an "incarnate" vision of God.

James goes on to add the bit about keeping oneself without stain from the world. "The world" was a widely used expression in the New Testament (especially in John's Gospel and Epistles) to refer to a way of thinking that is universal but contrary to the perspective and spirit that we have received from Jesus. "Keeping oneself without stain" is not about ritual purity or religious practice or moral law keeping. It's about Jesus' perspective of reality. What keeps that alive in us is the proper function of religion. But it also requires us to practice our religion in the same spirit.

Thus in the Community there was an integration of secular and religious life in which each had an effect on the other. In normal church life, there is often an expectation that a church service will "do something" for the participants. They want to be inspired and refreshed, and are often disappointed when it doesn't happen. In community life there is little of this expectation. Offices and services are just part of the routine; they affect life not by being dynamic, interesting or challenging, but by soaking the participants in the regular rhythm of worship and hearing the word of God. Just as in ordinary life members are careful of one another, so in religious services great care is taken over preparation and performance.

The overall effect is to live the sacred and the secular as one life, and this is what was really meant by not being "Sunday" Christians. In normal life the two tend to be kept in separate compartments, and this is one reason why there is pressure to make services relevant or interesting—they have to make up for a deficit in secular life during the rest of the week. But in community there is no difference between attending an office and setting the table for dinner. Both are daily happenings. Yet there is still more to it than this.

In normal life the pattern for most people is to live one's life in the world, so to speak, and to go to church on occasions as appropriate. In community, this pattern is reversed. Life is lived in the church, and it is from there that people go out into the world, say to a secular job. This was seen, not simply as an organizational arrangement, but as a spiritual kind of life. In it, the secular was sanctified by the sacred, that is, all of life was holy, not just the religious bits, and the sacred was humanized by the secular, that is, it served the needs of ordinary life rather than controlling it from a religious point of view. This meant that community life was very human and forgiving; it was not dominated by religious rules and dictums. On the other hand the worship of the Community was enhanced to an extraordinary degree because it was a corporate act, not a performance that people merely attended.

Of course, "living life in the church" is, almost by definition, a corporate affair, although because it is a spiritual life it is not necessarily tied to any particular structure. Monastic communities maintain a witness to it, but the particular genius of the Community of Celebration was that it made that kind of spiritual life accessible to families and children.

Chapter 14

Prayer

Some form of corporate daily prayer was the foundation of community life from the very earliest beginnings in Houston. The original group had met together to pray and study the scriptures. Graham Pulkingham had taught that those who gathered together in this way were to be "a people of praise." Prayer and worship were at the heart of everything that happened.

When the Community of Celebration was formed at Yeldall Manor, daily prayer and worship took the form of "chapel" at the end of the working day, attended by children and adults. It was a family time with much singing and story telling. Later on, as the years went by and long term vocation began to emerge, a pattern of daily offices was established. The practice took time to develop, but eventually settled into a routine of Morning, Noonday and Evening Prayer, occasionally with Compline, and a weekly Eucharist also celebrated on major saints' days.

At Cumbrae, where the primary transition took place from a "charismatic happening" to a community modeling itself on religious orders, the needs of the situation led to a rather more contemplative style of prayer. It was normal for people to take one day retreats. Fr. Roland Walls of the Community of the Transfiguration was a strong influence in this direction. He emphasized the importance of silence, stillness and solitude.

The Community at that time was extremely busy with the demands of ministry and with the maintenance of life. It was easy to feel there was no time for silence, which appeared to be totally unproductive. Roland Walls taught that it was, in fact, essential to the health of the Community. Listening to God took time, more time than would be spent on normal prayers, and it was an essential element in spiritual formation.

The Community responded to the challenge instinctively. One of its members, Patricia Allen, a Southern Baptist by background, began to sense a call to spend more time alone with God. Longer retreats eventually led to a fully fledged vocation as a solitary. It took very careful handling by Roland Walls, as any such vocation will do, but it was a genuine calling. Longer retreats eventually led to taking up residence in one of the monks' huts in the grounds of the cathedral at Cumbrae.

It was not easy for the Community, for Pat (as she was then known) had been a talented member of the Fisherfolk with strong relationships in the Community and also in the locality. Her withdrawal was described by people at the time as a kind of death. But she was not completely cut off. She remained fully part of the Community and supported by them as a praying presence at its heart. Today, Patricia lives in Israel as a solitary and continues to pray for the Community and its children.

Roland Walls designed a theological course for Community members, of which he was the tutor. The idea was that a small group would be trained initially, who would then take over the task of tutoring the rest of the Community. The aim was not to instill academic or theological knowledge as such, but to enable the Community to reflect theologically about its own life and experience. It was an important element of the new contemplative dimension.

This reflective process had significant consequences for the Community's outlook and its witness. The island of Cumbrae is situated in the Firth of Clyde, which was the approach to the

Polaris submarine base at Faslane. The presence of nuclear weapons in such close proximity was prime material for reflection on "kingdom" principles. Often Community members went on marches and demonstrations. Connections were established with many others in the worldwide peace and justice movement. Such connections were more than just a coming together of kindred spirits. They were seen as crucial to the spiritual health and development of the Community.

Although the Community had always had a special concern for those in need, prayer and contemplation under Roland Walls' guidance moved this beyond pastoral concern into a deeper understanding of the social and political dimensions of the gospel.

Other developments, too, were affecting the Community's experience of prayer. The long term personal and relationship issues that arose through living together had led to various experiments and exploration, particularly in association with Frank Lake at Post Green. His work on Primal Therapy opened up repressed psychological wounds that needed an appropriate path towards healing. Conventional prayer ministry might well be helpful at this point, but the situation also led naturally to the need for silence and to a variety of meditative techniques and the use of art as a form of prayer. Such techniques came to be seen as useful not only as an aid to healing but also, more generally, as a means of spiritual growth and development.

Charismatic worship tends to be monochrome. It looks and sounds pretty much the same everywhere. It uses the same kind of language; it has the same expectations; it has the same picture of God. It is to be expected that "following the Spirit" will lead to greater variety, but that does not mean it is easy to integrate different forms. In the church at large people tend to stick with the forms that they know, which is one reason why it is often hard to bring together charismatic worship with the worship of peace and justice movements.

Sticking with one form means getting used to it, feeling uncomfortable with something different. This shapes the human spirit in such a way that it can sometimes feel almost as if someone from a different background or tradition is practicing a different religion. It becomes hard to communicate sympathetically. It was important to the Community's development, as well as its ministry, that it was able to embrace a whole spectrum of prayer.

By "spectrum" is meant the range of practice, in broad terms. At one end of the scale, so to speak, is contemplative prayer, prayer that is stillness, without words. In the middle are the familiar forms of prayer, which use words in one form or another. At the other end is prayer that uses a form of language but which is unintelligible, i.e. speaking in tongues. Most people think of prayer as intelligible communication with God, but this range of practice shows, at the extremes, that prayer is on a different plane from verbal activity.

Prayer uses words, but words are not essential. It uses the mind, but mental activity is not essential to it. This is because prayer is a *spiritual* activity: it comes from within. Prayer is the activity of God, who is Spirit. We are told that the Holy Spirit "intercedes for us." In the creation story, when God says, "Let there be light," that is the activity that we call prayer. Jesus taught that prayer releases the spiritual power of the kingdom of God into the world. It is not simply verbal communication; it is a creative spiritual force.

By embracing different kinds of prayer, the Community held itself open to the creative possibilities involved in following the Spirit. Its corporate life ensured that integration took place rather than division into special interest groups. Over time, there might be a waxing or waning of some kinds of prayer, according to the situation and the needs. But in general there was a feeling that spiritual life had been shaped by a variety of different kinds of prayer, rather than just one tradition.

One form of prayer implicit in the life was intercession. Intercession is often thought of as verbal prayer of a certain kind, often the prayer of individuals who have a particular burden for some need. But the basic principle of intercession is identification with the person or need prayed for. Thus Christ brought the life of God into the world, identified himself with humanity, endured the pain of that encounter and carried that pain before God. It was his suffering that made him an intercessor, not verbal praying, even though he may have done plenty of that.

The principle of identification in the Community's case was identification with modern secular life whilst at the same time trying to live by the principles of the kingdom of God — and experiencing the pain that could bring, in terms of frustrated ambitions, absence of material prosperity and so on. All of this was brought before God in its worship. Hence, at a certain level, prayer, worship, faith and action all merged into almost the same thing. It all added up to a single life, participated in by all who lived it. Like a tree with several branches, there is a point where all these categories are undifferentiated, because they are all part of the same trunk.

Chapter 15

Faith

Faith is a slightly slippery subject, because it means different things in different contexts. In its broad sense, it refers to a set of theological concepts and the religious practices that go with them. Thus we speak of the Christian faith, or of various faith communities. The word is often used in the context of social and political witness, to refer to a response to the biblical imperative to establish justice and peace.

In my background it also had more personal meanings. First there was trust in Jesus for salvation, which was intimate and personal and had relatively little element of risk. Then there was belief that God would answer prayer. This was a difficult subject, because it didn't necessarily happen. Hence it often seemed to me that, despite many claims, when it came down to it not many people were prepared to take serious risks on the basis of faith.

The roots of the Community of Celebration were in the charismatic movement of the 1960s and 1970s, which held out the prospect of a God who was more real than we had previously experienced. In that environment it was expected that miracles happened. People looked for God to intervene directly in human affairs in much the same way as reported in the Bible, or at least in the New Testament. Many stories seemed to bear this out, though it was also partly a question of expectations. In a certain kind of spiritual atmosphere things happened, and where there was a heightened awareness of God people developed the confidence of faith.

In community, faith meant rather more than the expectation of divine intervention such as in healing ministry. While it might be the case that a minister had to rely on God to act in a ministry situation, at the Church of the Redeemer it was also likely to mean relying on God for personal security. Hence it was one thing to give God the credit for remarkable healings; quite another to have sufficient confidence in God's care to make oneself totally vulnerable where money and possessions were concerned.

For example, in pre-Celebration days at the Church of the Redeemer, some who worked full time at the church were dependent on designated gifts—there was no central source of funding. One member told a story of having no money to buy groceries or washing powder, a necessity with a baby in the house. A visit to the church confirmed that there were no designated funds, but on return home a large bag of groceries was sitting on the doorstep, including a big packet of washing powder. Such incidents helped to build faith, but also established a deeper dimension to "trusting God" than was typical in church life.

Thus faith was not a static concept, like relying on a source of income. God was not just one of many possible resources to help you get through life. Faith was a *response* to God. You did not choose to live by faith because it was a possible life option. You did it as a response to the God whom you encountered in your spiritual walk. In that process, you discovered what it really means to believe.

It was not uncommon, amongst a certain constituency of community supporters, to tell similar stories of God providing just enough money in the nick of time. The implication seemed to be that this is the way God works, for those willing to trust him. But a black South African member at Post Green in the days of apartheid put this issue in perspective very simply. At that time there were plenty of "charismatics" in the white South African church, and stories of God answering prayer in this way abounded. Our member from South Africa said, "How come God answers white folks' prayers for money, but not those of blacks?" It was a fair point. God is supposed to hear the cry of the poor but in this case seemed more disposed to listen to the petitions of the rich. It seemed clear that something else was going on here that had little to do with God but a lot to do with social and religious context.

In community, faith became a different world view. "Living by faith" involved more than trust in God to supply needs. It did not mean God was constantly intervening to smooth the path. Jesus himself used extreme language to anyone who would follow him, talking about "counting the cost," or "taking up your cross." In relation to money, his attitude seemed to be, "Live for today; don't worry about tomorrow." In a modern world of careers, salaries, financial commitments, pensions and insurance, that sounded like subsistence living, but it was less about the level of material resources than the principle: "be content with what you have." Don't spend all your energies avoiding trouble. In the last resort, as Jesus showed, it meant being content for one's life to be in God's hands with no guarantee that God would save it.

It followed from this that faith was essentially a community matter. In ordinary church life it was often hard to grasp this, given that we live in an age of individualism that is also deeply entrenched in our religious belief system.

A life of faith cannot normally be lived in full apart from the community of faith. Even in cases where people have received gifts in answer to prayer, clearly such a life cannot exist apart from a community of faith in which others see it as part of their Christian service to give. In community the principle of faith (or at least one of them) was sharing. That meant many people were able to work full time in the Community with no salary. It also meant potential vulnerability if and when money producing community members moved on. But that was the meaning of faith. "What if it all breaks up in five years?" was one of the questions posed in Britain in the early days. The answer was that it might very well do so, but those who put themselves in that vulnerable position would just have to trust God for that if it arose.

Faith understood as a different world view stretches well beyond personal experience. A world view encompasses the social fabric, including the shared assumptions on which social, political, and cultural practices are based. Christian alternatives to what the secular world offers tend to produce enclaves of Christianity for the faithful to withdraw from the world and spend time with each other, or else they are basically propaganda centers. The one thing they do not seem to do is to challenge the status quo of our culture; in fact, they look no different from it. They give the impression that in terms of human life generally faith only scratches the surface. Hence a Christian enterprise might adopt ethical practice, but it would not normally challenge the basis of the capitalist system itself and everything that flows from it.

How would one critique a system such as capitalism from the standpoint of the faith of Jesus? After all, the church itself, and every individual Christian, are subject to it. Faith requires that we understand where we are coming from, and how that relates to what we have received from Jesus. It is very difficult to come to that understanding, in relation to a social system, when we are part of it ourselves. Often it is necessary to step outside it, to live life according to a different set of premises, in order to see it more clearly. This was one of a number of reasons for living in community, which certainly did that.

The difference in economics was obvious. Shared income meant that everyone got the same, from the most senior leader down to the youngest child. The level of per capita income was well below what most people would regard as normal, due to economies of scale, sharing, recycling and making do. The need for fewer wage earners meant that people normally forced to spend a large proportion of their lives in employment could be released for other kinds of work. There was a counter-intuitive social effect. It is often imagined that community life squelches individual identity in the name of the corporate. In fact, the absence of a key determinant of social inequality, income differential, meant that individuals had a higher value and gained a sense of identity and belonging.

Aside from economics, many cultural norms were confronted by community life. Often the effect of these norms is to identify the acceptable and the unacceptable and to avoid the necessity of working out differences. They create distance between people. Take, for example the famous British stiff upper lip. There is nothing particularly "Christian" about that; it originates from a period of British history when stoicism in the face of hardship was considered a virtue, typified by such iconic figures as Scott of the Antarctic. Today it comes across as hard, cold, unfeeling and unapproachable. But in community life the demands of faith made it imperative to deal with what it is to be human. Hence people were encouraged to express their feelings—especially men. There was no virtue to be gained from hiding behind a mask.

Community life confronted deep-seated issues such as gender, race and sexuality with an immediacy that was not normally possible in ordinary church life. Even so, they were not easy to deal with. It was several years into this way of living before women were fully acknowledged as leaders. The Community never really got to grips with race, though the presence of one or two black members certainly provoked vigorous discussion. It was a long time before gay members felt free to acknowledge who they were, though it was not really a secret and certainly did not affect their participation in community life.

In all these matters, what happened in the Community mirrored developments elsewhere; but whereas the church often had extreme difficulty in dealing with them, for the Community it was a question of faith. Faith had to do with the kind of humanity that reflects the Spirit of God rather than with laws and traditions. It required serious engagement with the assumptions we bring to religious, social and political beliefs.

Community life confronted what is perhaps the most deep-seated human value of all, that of independence. Individualism is one of the defining aspects of our age, only deepened by the loss of centeredness that we call post-modernism. In the church, it has very long roots, going back to the Reformation. The result is a kind of me-and-God spirituality, which frees me to do more or less as I see fit, subject only to broad social rules. It is not necessarily a bad thing. It challenges injustices that arise through the imposition of values and cultural norms—often based on deep-seated prejudices, vested interests and methods of social control, which can apply in the church as much as in secular society. But the down side is loss of genuine community and insistence on personal rights, a pervading spirit of the times that seems to deepen the sense of alienation rather than lessen it.

It is often felt that the only alternative to this is a return to social control and absolute values (i.e. values imposed by external authority), but faith is not about social control *or* doing your own thing. Faith is a spirit that respects who we are as individuals whilst also recognizing our connectedness and the basis for it. For Christians it is tempting to locate the basis for our connectedness in God, but in practice it is difficult to separate God from our humanity. If we do, we set up some other basis for connectedness such as a doctrine or shared belief. But God is revealed through faith, which is demonstrated when we refuse to allow *anything* to separate us from one another. Of course, all this is much easier said than done. In practice, it is a struggle. But the church needs that kind of perspective if it is to bring Christian faith to bear on the social and spiritual undercurrents of today. Living in community was a practical way for ordinary people to explore the dimensions of faith.

Chapter 16

The Bible

The Bible was never a source of controversy in the Community, despite a wide range of theological backgrounds among its members. If anyone were to insist on a particular interpretation of scripture it might have been problematic, but in general it was possible to use the Bible as a source of inspiration for spiritual life without getting enmeshed in contentious issues.

In the church at large it was a different matter. The status and authority of the Bible was a highly contentious issue, and today the situation is so polarized that a single remark can instantly label a person as belonging to one camp or another. Here, the everyday human reality of life in Christ often sits in the background. The important issue is perceived to be whether or not one conforms to a particular religious outlook or ideology.

Labeling, however, is diametrically opposed to the community spirit. Since those who joined the Community of Celebration did so in response to a movement of the Spirit, it followed that the spirit of community life was more important than theological prejudice. This allowed people of quite different viewpoints to live together in peace, even using the Bible together as a source for Christian discipleship. It was one of the most encouraging things about charismatic renewal.

Charismatic religious language often looks and sounds quite similar to evangelical language. This may have made it easier, initially, for some to adapt to Bible sharing in the Community, but the real challenge was not in biblical interpretation. In Bible sharing the principle was that of listening to God in the other. All the contributions were gathered up into a summary, which became God's word for the group that day.

This implied that scripture was for the benefit of the body rather than for individuals, though it was important that individuals study it for themselves. It was to be expected that God worked through the body, supported by the Bible as it was studied and reflected on together. Here the relationship between "the Spirit" and the scriptures was likely to be much clearer than in an individual case. Jesus' parables, for instance, usually made much more sense when considered in a corporate setting. They did not instruct so much as illuminated what was already happening in common life. Their function was to deepen spiritual understanding of what the Community's life was about.

This naturally cut across deeply ingrained patterns of relating to Christianity in a very personal and individualistic way, but it also subverted the notion of the Bible as either a kind of oracle or a manual of doctrine. Some visitors, for example, wanted to know if community living was *justified* by scripture, or whether the Community considered it be *required* by the scriptures. In truth, the Community never related to its life in that way. Rather, there was a dynamic interaction between the Spirit and scripture, in which the Bible both inspired and illuminated what people were moved by the Spirit of God to do.

This process was so creative and life giving that it took the Bible out of the mental straightjacket that allowed only one way of interpreting it. It also made it possible, over time, to look at a number of related issues without compromising faith, even if they were highly controversial in the church at large. But the dynamic was lost as soon as the Bible was separated from the context of a life being lived by the Spirit, or when "Bible" and "Spirit" were effectively pitted against each other in a kind of hierarchy.

One of the huge issues in the church, never more so than in the post-modern cultural context, is the question of authority for matters of belief and behavior. If the ultimate source for this is located in the Bible, usually there is some sort of definitive framework of doctrine with boundaries that cannot be crossed. Scholarly investigation of the Bible is accepted because of its power to illuminate in a world shaped by a scientific outlook, but rejected where it goes beyond the boundaries. This illustrates the problem.

The Bible is a collection of different types of documents written over several centuries. It is not definitive enough to be a final authority, unless a theological scheme is imposed on it—which it is possible to do, but then it is the ideology rather than the Bible itself which is the real authority. Historical narrative, for example, is often invested with authority because there is a lot riding on it—it gives religious truth the appearance of objective truth as opposed to myth. But the fact is that history cannot provide the certainty required by religion; they are two different subjects. Scholarship is actually neutral as regards faith. It is a discipline, which is subject to the rules that govern those kinds of pursuits, and is compromised when its procedures are "bent" in the service of prejudice, whether faith or unbelief.

In reality, the factual accuracy of biblical statements is rarely an issue for religious life or faith. Whether Jesus really walked on water makes little difference; true or not, the moral of the story in countless sermons will be a religious truth having nothing to do with water or the suspension of the laws of physics. What some Christians prefer is a closed system of belief—in the case cited above, for example, belief that Jesus is the Son of God and belief that he walked on water are all part of a single package. There is something to be said for this approach, which has no reflection on intelligence. It has the advantage that it can generate a high degree of commitment and moral integrity. But in Community life, a closed system was inappropriate unless everyone were to belong to the same church and adopt the same theology.

Having been brought up in a closed system myself, I was well aware of its fundamental weakness, namely that if any part of it were shown to be incorrect, the entire belief system could potentially fall like a house of cards. This produced a predisposition to defend it, which was easily confused with faith. But I was also aware of the quality of spiritual life that those beliefs were capable of sustaining. That was the core that was important — not the eccentricities of belief, but that which came from a heartfelt response to God.

To "follow the Spirit" meant that the walls of division between people — whatever they were — were broken down. This was a primary experience of God, happening in real time, independent of any biblical injunction yet at the same time informed and fueled by study of the Bible. It was quite a different dynamic from the closed system, where the Bible is assumed to promote conformity to expected norms. In this dynamic, distinctions such as "conservative" or "liberal" were meaningless.

In putting stress on the simple sayings of Jesus, attention was drawn in the Community to the fact that the real authority for Christian belief and behavior was Jesus himself. This includes the way in which the relationship between Spirit and scripture is worked out. In a closed system, it is simply assumed that the Spirit will never promote anything other than the expected norms of a given theological viewpoint. The real situation, as Jesus showed, is less tidy and more challenging.

Most of what Jesus said was "by the Spirit," that is he was talking about spiritual life rather than abstract principles. He was quite free about citing scripture, reinterpreting it or even setting it aside. When he did so, frequently the result was inclusion rather than exclusion, making room for people who would otherwise be marginalized. The closed system of his own religious milieu found it extremely difficult to cope with this, but it was the model he left for his disciples.

To "follow the Spirit" is simply another way of talking about trying to live by the Spirit of Jesus. It was inevitable that this would affect attitudes to the Bible as it did many other things. In the present climate, if you are in not in one camp you are assumed to be part of another. But Jesus defied labels; he was neither conservative nor liberal. The context for his religious life was a life given to God in a real way, as opposed to a self protective or self serving way. Thus he could talk about fulfilling the law in the same breath as laying it to one side when he saw it to be necessary.

Hence the relationship of Spirit and scripture is not an intellectual question of setting one above the other in a kind of hierarchy, nor is it a kop out that allows biblical injunctions to be ignored. To follow the Spirit of Jesus ultimately leads to a cross if one pursues it far enough, so the context for this relationship is dynamic. It is not the milieu of academia or coffee table discussion.

In Community life, the Bible was not a rule book; it was a treasury of timeless wisdom. Just as the authority of God is very broad (Jesus spoke of a mansion with many rooms) so the Bible reflects the same breadth, making room for many different kinds of people who find inspiration in its pages. Eventually, the way in which that wisdom was assimilated in community life was through daily offices rather than through corporate Bible sharing.

This did not eliminate personal Bible study, but it created a rhythm in which the Bible was allowed to speak for itself. Over a period of time (months and years) it sank into the soul, informing spiritual life. But the dynamism of the Spirit–scripture relationship in early years lingers on in the corporate memory. The Community today remains hospitable to people of different persuasions and is quite resistant to theological labels.

Chapter 17

Evangelism

"Believe on the Lord Jesus Christ and you will be saved" (Acts 16.31). That was the traditional evangelistic message of my youth, or if you prefer the more sugar coated version devised by Bill Bright of Campus Crusade for Christ, "God loves you and has a wonderful plan for your life." In the latter version at least, the message is essentially a personal one about the transformation of individual lives through placing trust in Jesus.

The reality in many churches is that people come to faith by a process of osmosis. They are brought up in the church or they absorb its message through attendance at its services and activities. For its part the Community did not hold evangelistic services as such, nor did it take over the role of churches in basic Christian teaching. But it was, nevertheless, profoundly evangelistic in its manner of life.

The evangel simply means good news, and while the *content* of the good news today usually involves a religious message about Jesus, the gospel that Jesus preached himself had a rather wider application. He preached that the kingdom of God had arrived, which by definition was good news at every level. So the message was a proclamation about liberation, acceptance, healing and forgiveness, all of which Jesus substantiated by the way he went about his ministry, challenging the status quo as well as ministering to personal needs.

Whatever view one takes about Jesus' religious significance, part of "believing in him" is to believe the message that he preached—which in turn means making it concrete. Thus evangelism cannot be separated into a special compartment as a verbal religious message, notwithstanding the phenomenon of mass evangelists who have often been spectacularly successful in doing just that.

For Jesus, the gospel was a complete package. No distinction was made between a verbal message and an action, between spiritual and material deliverance, or between personal and social or political liberation. A good example is the story of Jesus' dealings with the man let down on his bed through the roof. Jesus says to him, "Your sins are forgiven," and then later tells him to get up and walk. When challenged by the onlookers, he replies, "Which is easier, to say 'Your sins are forgiven,' or to say 'Get up and walk?'"

The onlookers' response was that only God can forgive sins, and the natural *religious* response today might well be much the same. But where the gospel is a package there is no difference between telling someone their sins are forgiven and telling them to be healed. Whether they were slaves to sin or bound by infirmity or oppressed by injustice, it was all the same to Jesus. The issue was the gospel, not his qualification to forgive sins.

The evangelistic message today often sounds conditional: believe in Jesus and your sin will be forgiven. Jesus was unconditional.

Contrary to accepted belief, God welcomes everyone, right down to the lowest of the low — in fact, *especially* the lowest of the low. God makes no distinctions on the basis of social class or contribution to society or moral behavior, and forgiveness of sins is without conditions. Believing this transforms human relationships and results in acts of healing and liberation. Jesus' message clearly got through to some of his hearers, if not to the opinion makers. We read that "the common people heard him gladly."

Hence separating personal religious experience from the rest of life, and interpreting it in esoteric religious terms, distorts evangelism. It can have the result that some of the issues that Jesus tackled are hardly addressed in modern church life. At the heart of Community life was a desire to explore more fully what Jesus' gospel message was about, as reflected in his "simple sayings" — many of which seemed to have lost a lot of their potency in modern times.

Community life inevitably took a broader view than is often the case in more traditional evangelism. Evangelism and the gospel message were as much about "being with" and "standing alongside" as they were about "speaking to." The recipients of the good news were likely to be those with whom Christ identified himself rather than merely potential candidates for religious conversion.

In the Community, language and structures that seemed to imply some people were more faithful or more "spiritual" than others were avoided. There was a sense that community was a level playing field in that respect. Paradoxically, though the community was much more clearly defined than a church as to its boundaries, it was, for many, much easier to relate to. "Community" was just people, living ordinary life, yet there was nothing ordinary about the experience that many had. They were related to, on their own terms as human beings, as if they *mattered*. People would often speak of being "evangelized." The environment itself, rather than a kind of religious message, was the bearer of the evangel, the "good news."

With no partition of life into sacred and secular, no division between the "spiritual" side and the rest of life, it meant that all of life was sacred, including the dirty and unpleasant bits. One of the reasons such divisions are made, at least in people's minds, is because there is a desire to keep a holy place for God, protected from the earthiness of normal life. But that can have a profoundly counter-productive effect. It separates more than our earthy nature from God; it separates *us* from God. It can make us into religious, as opposed to godly, people, who think they have to get rid of their dirtiness in order to come near to God. It can obscure the gospel, because (despite protestations to the contrary) it conveys an impression that we are not good enough as we are to come to God. When there is no separation, it is the secular that is sanctified, that is, the reality of who we are, however unpleasant, is "accepted in the beloved."

In this perspective the material world is itself sacred, because that is where God is. In serving it, we serve God, not with undue reverence but with respect for what God created it to be. Human beings are part of that world, and it is their own collective "sin" — their fears, projections and so on — which makes it impossible for them to find a mirror that tells them who they are. The gospel, however — or at least the one according to Jesus — is that mirror.

Though the great majority of Community members were professing Christians, this kind of gospel was every bit as evangelizing as a conventional religious message. People were taken seriously, and for some of them it was the first time in their lives. This was the origin of the expression, often used in the Community: "evangelism by attraction."

Of course, the reality of community life, once people went into it, was often hard. Many things Jesus said and did caused a lot of offense and angst, whilst at the same time being experienced as liberation by others. So today: the things that dehumanize us are usually defensive ploys, and in community life they had to be addressed. No matter who you were, it was likely to be a painful process. But this did not alter the fact that, in general, community life was attractive and liberating.

No one church, or community, can fully reproduce the breadth of Jesus' gospel. It touches every aspect of human existence, individual, social and political. It is not simply a matter of *telling* people what the gospel is. It requires action to address issues that prevent people from hearing it. As Jesus explained and demonstrated what he meant, it became clear that, while it was good news for some, many aspects could not be achieved easily. Liberation for some was problematic for others, or in other areas of human life. The kingdom of God might look like normal social and institutional existence, but it was on a totally different plane spiritually. Consequently, those who had too much to lose, or who preferred to rely on violence and force to establish their picture of society, rejected its liberating principles. Jesus' message was "woe" to all such, for they would never experience the liberation of which the gospel spoke.

One example of an area desperately in need of liberation is our slavery to economics. It dehumanizes us and divides society. But realistically, is there any alternative? Jesus says freedom is possible, and in fact it is one of the characteristics of the kingdom of God, wherever it exists. It is a spiritual freedom, which can be expressed in all sorts of ways. It is perhaps not so much a question of equity as a spirit of generosity and of being content with what one has, thereby releasing resources for needs elsewhere. It sets us free to find ways of standing outside existing structures and gives us a clearer insight into the nature of the powers that govern all our lives—thereby making the prospect of creative solutions to problems of injustice thinkable.

Hence, this is also part of what "evangelism by attraction" is about. It is not about solving the world's economic problems. But it is about giving people a taste, if nothing more, of the freedom from the tyranny of economics that Jesus offers in his vision of the kingdom of God.

The power of money to control our lives is only one element addressed by Jesus' gospel of the kingdom. Another is security, the need to make sure that our personal position, or that of our nation, is protected as the number one priority. In the modern church little attempt is made, as a rule, to make the connection between security and faith. For educated Christians in a wealthy country, it is not always apparent that "faith" is underpinned not so much by God as by financial and other forms of security. In areas where people have next to nothing on which to rely for their safety or well being, faith is in God because they have nothing else on which to depend — a good reason why Christian faith in such countries often seems more vibrant than in the industrialized nations. But "security" is not a simple choice between God and money. In the world of Jesus security, like economics, always involves our relatedness to other human beings.

For Jesus, security is a function of interdependence rather than the sum total of assets. The value of family, for many people, is the assurance that there will be someone "there for me" when I really need it. That can mean anything from a listening ear to a place to live — and in the early days of Community life, it meant the whole range of such possibilities. It was not unknown, when someone came to the community in distress, to offer a simple solution: "come and live with us."

Security becomes more of an issue, the more *in*dependent we become. More and more energy goes into protecting and providing for our own situation — because if we don't, no one else will. Security raises the whole issue of vulnerability, and how we deal with it.

There are many other areas in which the liberating gospel message of Jesus needs to be heard. Cultural attitudes, for example, control the way many people think. Distinctions and divisions in society are another major subject desperately in need of "good news." Race, class and gender are typical of such divisions, but there are many others: age, disability, sexual orientation, education, ethnic origin or culture, religious belief. In all these areas, people find themselves disadvantaged to one degree or another for no reason other than the fact that they happen to fall into the wrong category.

While many of these subjects are debated and addressed in public life, it is another matter to experience the good news in relation to them. To get a sense of that we need to taste it, not talk about it or have it imposed upon us. One reason why the church often seems to lag behind society in moral and ethical matters may be because of the lack of a corporate life that is truly evangelistic in the way that Jesus' gospel was evangelistic.

The kingdom of God is "evangelizing." It does more than merely give us insight: it is actually experienced as freedom or liberation in all aspects of the human condition. It is, in other words, truly humanizing. The calling of those who believe Jesus' words is to make a taste of that life available. It can be only a taste, for the kingdom of God is far too vast a concept for our human limitations to contain. But like Jesus' picture of the leaven in the lump, its effects are incalculable. It is a spiritual way of being, once tasted never forgotten, so that its memory is carried into all manner of places and situations. That was the experience, still talked about, of many of those who have lived in the Community of Celebration over the years.

Chapter 18

Politics

The Community was not political in the way that some communities were — for example, the Sojourners Community in Washington DC. That is, it did not concentrate all its energies on political witness. However, it did maintain close links with a variety of communities involved in peace witness, and this was also reflected in its literature such as GrassRoots Magazine, published in the pre-1985 period. From time to time members of the Community participated in marches or acts of witness at sites such as the nuclear submarine base on the Clyde or Lakenheath air base in England. Such events were also common in Washington DC, and the Community often participated in these and still does to the present day.

Frequently the Community received visitors actively involved in other fields, some of whom, like Jim Punton of the Frontier Youth Trust or Alan Kreider of the London Mennonite Centre, developed an ongoing relationship with the Community with real input into its life. It was through such contacts that GrassRoots Magazine was developed at Post Green. Jeanne Hinton was its editor. Inspired by Sojourners Magazine, the publication of that community with whom there had been a connection for a number of years, it addressed a range of social and political issues. Although it did not survive the reorganizations of the mid-1980s, it was seen as a significant element of the "Celebration" ministry of Post Green and Cumbrae.

Hence although direct action is not the main focus of the Community, its life has been consistently informed politically through contacts and participation, through its prayer life and through the literature of the peace movements.

The foundation of the Community was such that it drew in a wide range of people from all sorts of theological backgrounds. It did not only attract the politically radical. Hence participation in forms of public witness was not compulsory, and the necessity for such events could be the subject of debate. Nevertheless, community life itself inevitably had an effect on everyone's political outlook. It meant, for example, that the concerns most people have, such as taxes and standards of living, were no longer much of an issue for Community members, and what became more important were the wider issues of justice and peace in the world.

Some Community members came from a church background in which religion and politics were separated. For them, it would have been natural to look to the Bible for guidance on how to connect the two, and finding no direct link would have felt free (in church life) to pursue religion in isolation, or at any rate to fulfill the Biblical command to care for the poor largely through charity or some form of ministry. In that, they were not untypical of western Christians.

In many churches life simply carries on from week to week with little acknowledgement of what is happening in the world at large, and this can easily generate an impression that politics is somehow an inappropriate subject for local church life. In the Community, such attitudes were not usually confronted directly. They were changed as a result of the life and the way it was talked about, and through interaction with many Community friends involved in peace and justice witness.

Modern life tends to obscure the fact that the world of Jesus was a religious society in which there was no separation of religion and politics, so in reality most of his sayings have a political as well as a personal dimension. This is probably why Matthew, for example, has Jesus commanding that the gospel be preached to "all nations" rather than to "all people." The separation of religion and politics is a very modern phenomenon; historically, religion has always fulfilled a social and political role.

In early centuries Christianity was very attractive to slaves, and it was persecuted in part because it was a focus of spiritual resistance to the power of the secular state. In British history one only has to think of Methodism and its success in giving an identity to the emerging artisan class. In America, the "religious right" is a clear example of religion and politics coming together to articulate the felt needs of a section of society. Other cases might include the role of the missionary movement in spreading western culture, or the function of liberation theology in giving voice to South America's poor.

In community, the political imperative stems from the fundamental concept of God as a God of mercy and justice. It is also informed by the injunction to serve Christ in the poor — a very easy concept to understand in the highly relational context of community life. In church life generally, while there may be differences of emphasis (for example, charity or political action), in practice there are often specific issues that for a time act as a focus for a broad range of Christian opinion and activity. Examples in the Community's history included the campaign for nuclear disarmament and the anti-apartheid movement, both of which engaged people at more than a theoretical level and helped shape both religious and political outlook.

Such engagement goes deeper than the specifics of the issue in question. The driving force of politics is ideology, and there is no agreement amongst Christians as to whether they should be on the left or the right. Both positions are likely to be criticized from a Christian point of view, yet Christians cannot avoid ideology by concentrating on limited issues which command broad agreement. For instance, in the west we all live in a market economy and abide by its assumptions (mostly without protest) every day, whatever we may think about capitalism. So Christians have to use ideology but need to be able to critique its assumptions. Community life was a constant reflection on the assumptions that underpin social and political life.

Even churches use ideology, though they may be very reluctant to use that word. Most churches are known as evangelical, liberal or middle of the road, and generally those who attend them abide by their ethos. Ideology is more powerful than our personal opinions; indeed, it forms them. But in community, the non-judgmental and inclusive character of the life meant that such labels could not be allowed to define relationships or control worship. Hence it was possible to stand outside them, at least to some degree.

Ideology frequently gets attached to a political agenda, both gaining in power by feeding off each other. Any theological statement has political implications, because theology has to do with God and therefore carries some sort of imperative in the way it is worked out in human life. A defective theology can be disastrous, as we have seen in the way it has been used to justify anti-Semitism or apartheid. Christian culture in the west has many roots in ideas derived from the church. Freedom, for example, is a Christian value, one that is not by any means estab-lished in the psyche of eastern cultures. So is the idea that each individual is a unique person. In many countries there is little concept of this, which is one reason why torture and human rights abuses are able to flourish there, and why democracy is not considered to be particularly desirable.

But theology includes a great many insights, which have to be kept in balance. Freedom, for example, is not an absolute value; we are also urged to serve Christ in the poor and to be content with what we have, the latter carrying with it environmental overtones as well as the need for justice. More generally, the Christian spirit is about laying down power, or empowering others, not about using it to one's own advantage or to enforce one's will. This may well conflict with prevailing values and political agendas derived from our own spiritual tradition.

For example, to many people it seems self-evident that western values are superior to those of Middle Eastern Islam. But there are many things about western culture that one could comment on from a theological point of view. Jesus' truth is not imposed at the point of a gun. It is not imperialistic, seeking to dominate others to its own advantage. Western culture is materialistic, empty, hedonistic, militaristic, imperialistic, exploitative both of the environment and of nations, and often seems to have little concern beyond the unlimited accumulation of wealth. Theology has a great deal to say about all of this. The life of Jesus in the world is always going to be salt, either seasoning or disinfectant; it will never be pure ideology. Christians *may* have to make a choice between one ideology and another, in any given time and place, but they should always be ready to critique their own presuppositions and refuse to be bound by ideology's absolute demands.

Continuous political reflection thus becomes part of the imperative of faith. The function of faith is not to merely sanction culture but to critique its assumptions—including those of the faith community itself. Of course it is often easier to do that by stepping outside the cultural norms—which community life did, in many respects. One interesting result was the way in which some individuals of a conservative temperament found themselves expressing views that most would regard as politically radical.

The Community laid a lot of stress on the biblical image of the body of Christ, which was understood as a metaphor for real time human society (i.e. not just a mystical concept). It was central to the Community's self image and inevitably influenced its worldview. Thus political questions were seen from the standpoint of our relatedness as human beings rather than from ideology as shaped by religious belief. Religious ideology derives its authority and power from the fact that it is a matter of faith and is therefore not open to discussion, which should make anyone extremely cautious about defining as faith something that is really just a point of view. Maybe a speck is in someone else's eye but a plank is in one's own. All this holds in the religious world but it has its counterpart in the world of politics.

A good example comes from the cold war era. At the time prevailing political dogma in the west demonized the communist bloc as a threat to world peace. It was referred to as the "axis of evil." Politics was defined as a fight between freedom and tyranny. But while many people in the church simply went along with this dogma, Christian communities were prominent among those who saw the excesses of the freedom camp itself to be the real threat. In the name of freedom, stupendous sums of money were spent on weaponry that could destroy the world several times over. Governments that brutally oppressed their own people were supported, while others that had popular support were demonized. Notwithstanding input from many external sources, there is no doubt that the perspective of the Community of Celebration on these issues was significantly shaped and informed by its own internal life and self image as an expression of the body of Christ.

Today, the world has moved on, but the basic scenario is not dissimilar. The enemy today is Islamic fundamentalism. The same language has been used, of an "axis of evil." The way to combat it is through the spread of freedom and democracy, if necessary by force. In other words, there has developed the same "freedom versus tyranny," "good guys versus bad guys" scenario as existed in the days of the Cold War. The same ideological battle is being waged: there is the ostensible battle between western values and Islam, and another between those who would harness traditional religious beliefs to political (and self interested) objectives, and those who would challenge those same objectives from a Christian point of view. The linkage of religious and political ideology is always liable to generate an uncritical crusade, which is really no different in principle from that of the Islamic fundamentalist. "God" is simply assumed to be on one side or the other, without reference to those things by which we know God: justice, mercy, kindness, gentleness, longsuffering, denying oneself for the sake of others, and so on.

At the heart of the confrontation between the west and Islam remains the ongoing conflict in the state of Israel. This is an extremely difficult situation, but one that is bedeviled by ideology masquerading as justice. At its core it is a struggle for land between two peoples trying to establish nationhood, but western attitudes are colored by various subliminal feelings: an affinity for Israeli attitudes based on a shared Judeo-Christian culture, guilt about the Holocaust, political self interest and so on. In some sections of the church there is enthusiasm for a Zionist agenda based on millenarian predictions. Such ideological ideas command enormous power, to the extent that objective issues of justice can hardly be addressed. Here, the danger for Christians is that in the name of ideological religious belief the gospel of Jesus is simply stood on its head. This was often a topic for comment in community circles, for whom the spiritual imperative was to view a situation from the standpoint of the oppressed.

During the apartheid years, Archbishop Desmond Tutu made a famous remark. He said, charitably in the circumstances, that he was puzzled as to which Bible people were reading when they said religion had nothing to do with politics. He was reflecting a widely felt divide in the church at that time, which was also the context for political discussion in the Community. For the Community, especially in its early years, was but a microcosm of the church at large. There was a wide cross section of people, some of whom were actively involved in forms of political witness while others seemed to have little interest. What the Community did, however, was to make it possible for everyone to appreciate the political dimension of faith, and to explore it, whatever their individual calling to witness may have been. It did that simply by the character of its corporate life and its reflective process.

Chapter 19

Church

Not every Christian community sees itself as a church. Many are formed to promote a ministry or a cause, or for mutual support in following a rule of prayer. "Church" implies a full sacramental life and some form of accountability to the wider church of which it is a part. The Anglican Church recognizes basically two forms of church: open and closed congregations. Open congregations — the vast majority — are open to all and sundry. The closed congregations are the monastic religious communities. Just as a parish church is subject to the oversight of the bishop of the diocese, so is a religious community, usually by means of a visitor.

Initially the Community of Celebration did not fit entirely comfortably in this framework. It certainly had a sacramental life and saw itself as "church." It also saw itself as part of the Anglican Church and subject to its procedures. But it was not monastic. Its members took no vows and made no promises. They came and went almost as often as attendees at a local church—perhaps even more so.

There was also a certain amount of confusion as to its purpose. It had a powerful ministry promoting renewal of church life, but was that the reason for its existence? Did it exist as a form of church in its own right and for its own sake, or was it an agency, one of many that existed at the time, with its own particular sense of mission? If the latter, what was the aim, exactly? Was it to convert the rest of the church to Celebration's way of life?

It took years before the Community's vocation as a new form of religious community within the Anglican Church emerged and settled down.

It was talked about often enough, but the reality of it took a long time to come to terms with, especially as there were many people with strong ministry gifts whose contribution had the potential to skew the focus of the Community for a while. During this time there were attempts to provide teaching on the principles of community life, but for the most part they proved too difficult for churches to implement.

Nevertheless, the Community did have an underlying reason for its existence, which had something to do with bearing witness to the nature of church. The mission, as stated in its constitution, was to be "a sign of the celebration of life in Jesus Christ." Unlike the more traditional orders, which are a sign of the radical, disciplined life of Christ, Celebration's was a witness to the life of Christ expressed through the secular life of ordinary people, families and children. It therefore had something to say to the churches about their life together, as opposed to a message about personal holiness.

This was not a witness about church structures in the denominational sense. Despite a desire, particularly in early days, to rediscover the genius of Anglicanism, being "a sign of the celebration of life in Jesus Christ" had little to do with the mechanisms of church government or theological emphases that often lay at the root of denominational church structures. It was more to do with the spiritual nature of "church," particularly at the local level—something that in principle applied in any church, whatever its color.

Just as personal faith is not to do with practices and observances but fundamentally with who a person *is*, so the church is more than the sum total of its staff, organization and rituals.

It is a living organism, a spiritual entity — words which have no meaning unless they have some corresponding visible expression. People who are frustrated with the church are often searching for this spiritual core, in an inarticulate way as often as not, because they sense that in it they will find their own spiritual identity.

Contrary to the messages we all receive that tell us to think our own thoughts and do our own thing, this is what the church is for—to give us our spiritual identity. The ability of the Community to provide this for its members was one of the things that made it attractive.

It was one of the things that drew us to the Community, despite having belonged to a very lively church with a great deal going on. In church there was a subtle pressure to conform, in terms of both theology and social class. It was not intentional; it was probably just the nature of group dynamics. But it had the effect of training spiritual life like a plant being trained to grow in a certain way. Spiritual life does require discipline, but only in order to enable a person to be more fully who they were made to be. Conformity to the expectations of an institutional church or religious group does not set people free to be who they are, or give them a sense of their spiritual identity. The paradox is that we can only discover spiritual identity in relation to others, yet conformity can easily blind us to it.

Every Christian experiences the tension between structure and spiritual life. Some see this as a tension between the visible and the invisible church. The visible church is the church that we know, divided and containing all manner of people and beliefs. The invisible church is the company of all true believers, the saved known only to God, who are part of the visible church but not confined to it, and who, spiritually speaking, belong to no church but the mystical universal church of God. One problem with this outlook is that it encourages sectarianism, or at least withdrawal into narrowly defined theological enclaves. It produces forms of church that do not reflect the breadth of the Gospel: they neither witness effectively to the inclusiveness of God, nor are they salt and light in society. They are inadequate for the task of giving individual believers their true identity in Christ, and no matter how dynamic the spiritual impulse that brought them into being, over time they are seen to be as defective as the forms they replaced—or even more so.

The alternative is to view the church, with all its flaws, as a source of sacramental grace. The material world is a world of decay and renewal, a world of strengths and weaknesses. The individuals who make up the church cannot be models of sinless perfection. But it is this very world of imperfection that God in Christ has chosen to inhabit, and he does so, not by holding out an unattainable perfect alternative, but by becoming one with it in its imperfection. The manifest flaws of the church do not prevent it from being a source of grace for individual lives. By and large this is a reason for staying with the church that has formed us and abiding by its discipline. It is possible we will feel more comfortable elsewhere; but if we imagine that that will make us a better Christian, we are probably chasing an illusion.

Community life addressed the tension in two ways. First, it was understood that worship took place in the locality where you lived. Community members always attended the local Anglican Church, whatever type it was, rather than traveling to one that suited best. Second, its internal life transformed the cultural practice of "going to church." As the saying went, it was a move from living life in the secular world and going to church to living life in the church and going out to the secular world. In this way the Community confronted a consumerist attitude to religion that treated it almost as a commodity or service, like those offered by various institutions of society.

Of course, people who go to church are a mixed bag, and the nature of "church" is that it includes a role of "being there" for those who do not wish to make a full commitment to it.

Nevertheless, it remains the case that at the heart of Christianity there is a question of choice and commitment of one's life to God. The very existence of professional clergy is a testimony to this, and to the fact that it is the church's job to nurture and sustain it. But professionalism has its own dangers. It needs committed lay members yet it can easily stifle their giftedness. The fact is that many aspects of the modern clerical role are not intrinsic to the nature of church, but a disciplined, given-to-God life *is* at the core of it, and it is not the prerogative of a clerical caste.

One of the attractions of community life was directly related to this truth. Many ordinary people wanted to give their lives to God and needed a milieu in which to do it. By and large, the only avenue available in the church was the professional ordained ministry, a specialized vocation likely to appeal only to a minority. Community life provided the opportunity for full time Christian life and ministry without the necessity of ordination. Significantly, as numbers grew smaller, many former members did decide to pursue ordination—a much higher proportion, in fact, than one would expect from a normal church congregation, thus showing that at the core of "church" are committed lives. They do not have to be ordained, but if that is the only avenue available, that is the route they will go. Conversely, it also showed how ordination could be a bottleneck.

The non-parochial nature of community meant that priests in the Community did not have the burden of parish duties, though most did help out in local churches. Within the community, their role was reduced to almost that of a functionary, not by specific design or policy, but because when it comes to it there are very few things that can only be done by a priest.

The idea, prevalent in many churches, that it's the clergy's job to say grace at common meals, is a far cry from community life. Even at the Eucharist, it was normal in early days for the presiding role to be shared between a lay and an ordained member. Most of the ordained members were happy to accept a functional role while they were there, since other aspects of their lives were being developed, though it was inevitable over time that vocation would reassert itself. In this context many members were able to develop ministry skills that could never have emerged through normal life and ordinary church attendance.

Thus one way in which the Community addressed the tension between the institution and the needs of personal spiritual growth was by effectively dismantling the system of "one person ministry." (The flip side to this, of course, in a normal church setting, would also require that clergy be fully supported in their institutional responsibilities. This happened at the Church of the Redeemer.) By blurring the distinction between ordinary life and church life, it made it possible to make room for many different kinds of people. Sharing life is an earthy business, and there is nothing in a minister's training that makes him or her uniquely qualified to be a leader in it.

The Christian spirit is manifest primarily in the spirit with which ordinary life is lived, not by constantly drawing attention to religious truth. Yet without understanding of what is involved, spiritually and practically, in creating such a milieu, the chances are that separation of religious and secular life will happen by default, to the detriment of both. A church may appear to be a hive of religious activity, yet the things it does are seen by everyone, believers and unbelievers alike, to be just that—religious activity. The real genius of "church"—living sacred and secular as one life—is hidden.

The real church is attractive, to most people, because it appeals to humanity. Everyone wants friends, a supportive environment, a sense of community and belonging, a milieu of tolerance and acceptance, freedom from the worst aspects of competitiveness and acquisitiveness, a safe environment for children and so on. The church loses its value to the extent that such things are only available as part of a religious package, or available on a Sunday morning but not during the rest of the week.

The "kingdom of God" is a concept far wider than any church, yet the church needs to be a visible demonstration of its truths. This is not religious, propositional truth but visible, self evident truth, truth that all human beings instinctively recognize and trust because it accords with their understanding of what it is to be human. This is a long way from the "all welcome" message erected outside certain churches, which invite people to cross a threshold and join total strangers in an activity they know little about.

Within churches, life is governed by institutional needs. There are buildings to maintain, services to be run, missions to be supported. There are committees and procedures to be followed. Traditions powerfully control what goes on in many churches, from "this is the way we do things here" to theological traditions and forms of churchmanship. But the *spiritual* entity "church" is characterized by mutual love and a unity that is inclusive —not restricted to those of a like mind or type.

Paul's image of the body is a spiritual metaphor, but it is all too often taken to refer to jobs and roles rather than to personal identity — a typically institutional model. Since the institution can only give significance to roles, it is hardly surprising that people do not feel affirmed in their identity if they are told that their job as a floor sweeper is "just as important" as that of the leader of the church — and especially not if, as often happens, there is no outlet or respect for their real giftedness.

Jesus offered a great many images to help people visualize the kingdom of God. One, for example, was the pearl of great price, which a merchant sold all that he had in order to get. What we give up could be anything from possessions to beliefs and preju-dices, but the point is that these are words for today, not some ideal world of the imagination. So selling up for the pearl could often be seen, in community, as a metaphor for embracing common life — a different approach from seeing it in terms of biblical principles and obligations.

"Church" is not supposed to be a society of people who wear haloes. It is a place where people can be themselves whilst at the same time living the truths of the gospel. And the gospel is easy, so far as ordinary everyday living is concerned: there is no rat race and there is room for everyone. There *is* a cost, inasmuch as shared life involves sacrifices, but that is what you pay for the pearl. This was the spiritual truth of "church" that the Community made visible.

In the end, spiritual truth requires lives to make it real, and this is why the Community eventually modeled itself on a religious order. But obviously it is not possible — or desirable — to propose that churches structure themselves formally as communities. That would simply be another form of institution, which will ultimately define who people are and how they behave. The implications of community for churches have less to do with structure than with spirit, which can take many concrete forms.

What then does building "church" require? It certainly takes lives, committed to God, to place and to one another. It is not a job, like the clergy or even unpaid posts such as a lay reader. "Church" is the spiritual milieu that enables individuals to actually do what Jesus said, rather than privatizing their faith. That takes ordinary people's lives, given to one another as a matter of calling.

The purpose of lives given to one another is to address common features of our age with the truths of the gospel. These include the privatization of life and religion, issues of status and the related issues of inclusion. These are practical issues at the local level — there are many reasons why people feel they do not fit in or are not included — but they also have wider political dimensions that are often unseen and unfelt until they are confronted in real lives and relationships.

The church needs to be a resource for family life, not in the sense of telling people how to live their lives but providing them with resources and broad safe friendships. This is more than merely providing family services, which can cater for tastes in worship but can also reduce faith to the level of consumerism.

Several aspects of community life have highlighted money as a huge area in need of the gospel message. It is true that many churches encourage people to give sacrificially, but this is not about self denial. It is more about discovering the creativity that comes when we are set free from the control of this powerful force in our lives. A related issue is lifestyle and consumerism. The power of modern culture to suck in resources and isolate us from each other needs to be resisted. It is not a political resistance, necessarily, but a spiritual resistance—and it needs to be a positive experience for everybody. This is what "church" is for: to provide that experience in concrete ways, as opposed to merely articulating principles for individuals to pursue as they see fit.

The intellectual issues of the day need to be addressed. This is not an academic pursuit, though there may well be a need for such talents in the church. Rather, it is about ways of thinking that are so normal in the secular culture that their influence is hardly noticed in the church. For instance, the effects of postmodernist thinking are not dealt with by asserting the values of an older generation and condemning moral relativism. It is much better to demonstrate that Jesus showed how you could live a full and truly human life without the fear of what will happen to you if you do. He showed how you could trust God and live life as it comes, without being controlled by the fear that you won't get it right or you won't get what you want or you won't be able to pay the bills. That, in itself, is meaning, in a world that seems to have lost all sense of meaning. It is also good news.

There are no structures that will cause the church to deal with these issues merely by adopting them. But the Spirit will always find a way, and the hallmark of the Spirit is variety and creativity. That is what the Community tried to witness to, rather than a formal program of church renewal.

III A THEOLOGICAL JOURNEY

Chapter 20

God

To describe the Community's history as a theological journey
is in one sense a little misleading, for individual Community
members may or may not have seen their time in community in
that way, and certainly the Community itself has never had any
official doctrine beyond its adherence to Anglicanism.
Nevertheless, the series of developments that the Community
went through during a period of over 30 years amount to a
journey of sorts, a journey from an almost hippie style commune
to a small religious order. It would be surprising if there were not
some kind of theological progression along the way.

In the beginning the Community was the latest exciting development to hit the "renewal" scene. It came out of the charismatic
movement, which emphasized the importance of the Holy Spirit,
and initially at least looked hardly different from other groups
from the same stable. But while many such groups remained
fixed within that stream of consciousness, for the Community of
Celebration "following the Spirit" meant taking a track that
would ultimately diverge from the majority.

Community life undermined individualism at all sorts of levels,
including religious belief. People new to the Community generally
reflected the cultural patterns of society at large, which were
dominated by individualist thinking. Those from an evangelical
background may have had extra problems from a religious point of

view: for them God was primarily concerned with the individual, and therefore rights of private conscience and personal interpretation easily superseded those of corporate consciousness. But in general patterns of thinking were similar for everyone.

These patterns were so deeply entrenched that most were hardly aware of them. Thus the idea of seeing or hearing God in the other was radically new, especially when God was normally thought of as totally Other, a Being to be worshiped and obeyed privately in a very intimate and personal way. In this new community language, it seemed that God was also near, tangible and, in a way, negotiable.

For some this perspective also affected self image in subtle kinds of ways. In those days many people in the charismatic movement had an attitude to God that betrayed a certain anxiety. They were constantly asking God for guidance, as if God were a distant parent who had to be constantly summoned for help.

At Yeldall Graham gave a lot of pastoral teaching to the effect that if Christ is in you he is in every part of you, including your innermost thoughts. He is not some sort of alien being residing within you. Consequently you needed to be able to trust your own thoughts and decisions—because Christ was in them. You did not need to be forever asking for guidance. This linked with his teaching on Christian identity.

Although some individuals may have studied, for the majority there was no formal teaching of doctrine. But the life itself and the way it was talked about all had an effect on the way people thought about divinity. It depended on the context, but there was a distinct emphasis that often stood in marked contrast to the kind of religious language usually heard in churches. In whatever way God was spoken about—"God", "Jesus" or "the Spirit"—there was a characteristic "community" perspective that would slowly but surely affect theological outlook.

For Christians in general, "God" normally represents "what is over us," the one who calls out the instinct to worship, whether by life or by lips. In that respect Community theology was orthodox and traditional. Nevertheless, the awareness of God in real life did lead to a certain distinctive consciousness.

The idea of God as tangible, or "in" rather than "over" is of course an ancient part of Christian belief. It is more prominent in Catholic tradition than Protestant, emphasizing "being with" and seeing Christ in the poor, as opposed to "preaching to" and conversion of individuals. Hence in the Community there were originally some from the Roman or high Anglican tradition who might have felt more at home with Community jargon than others; but the charismatic movement certainly tended to encourage other worldly notions of God, and for many, there was no other model of God than the transcendent one—God was "out there" somewhere.

The technical word for God who is "in" is "immanent", not an easy idea for westerners to comprehend. One analogy might be to say that it is like color, i.e. you can't separate the color from the substance of which it *is* the color. And, if you want to press the analogy just a little further, if you are color blind you won't see it. This leads us to recognize and be aware of God in the ordinary world in which we live. But for many Christians there is a longing for something that takes you away, *out* of the ordinary, the dirty, the fallible and the temporary; in fact, part of the attraction of the charismatic experience was that it did just that. In community on the other hand it was necessary to learn how to see and hear God in each other—a rather different kind of experience.

Dealing with the reality of everyday life and relationships at close quarters required an awareness of God as present and palpable. It was largely a matter of perspective. When we become aware of God in real time, the experience is rarely a mysterious presence. Mostly it is conveyed through the use of certain words such as liberation, love, kindness, mercy, release, setting free, good news. People tend to regard these as *activities* of God, who is a person behind the scenes: displaying such characteristics at certain times when appropriate. But when the Bible says that "God is spirit" or "God is love," it is saying in effect that these things are of the very essence of God.

Hence to participate in these things is to participate in God. In relationships, for example, God is experienced in the process of reciprocity. The "given to" becomes the giver, in an endless cycle for which we use words like "friendship" or "love." There is not a one way street in which human beings are passive recipients of God's blessings. God is known when we are open to the other. Some may feel that their own interior encounter with God predominates over any other sense they may have of God's presence, but of course the problem with that is that private experience is by definition limited and is extremely vulnerable to self deception.

Unity in diversity is also a characteristic way in which we experience God. Unity is more than a matter of balancing the interests of otherwise divergent sets of people. It involves recognition of our belonging to one another, that in fact our interests are best served when they are understood in the context of that belonging. The Bible uses images such as the family or the human body to convey this. Diversity speaks of endless possibilities, which cannot be controlled by arbitrary limits. Yet it is not just a matter of saying "you have your ways and I have mine," but of recognizing that my life is not self sufficient without yours, and that I need to hold my beliefs or interests with a certain lightness of grip. I need to be open to being changed by who you are.

This is in marked contrast to the way in which religious affairs are commonly conducted, but when it happens, it may be felt as a direct experience of God. In the Community there was a powerful sense of belonging. It was not the belonging of a club, based on shared values or activities. It was the sense that you belonged because of who you were. You were respected by all, regardless of whether you were a church leader or someone who had just walked in off the street; regardless, too, of whether you were someone with special ministry gifts or just an ordinary person. This made it much easier both to listen and to be heard, and it was the most evangelistic tool in the community's locker, outweighing the things for which it was more famous, such as its style of worship.

Many people who joined the Community still had a fairly standard picture of God as an authoritative being who controlled their lives from the outside, as it were, according to his mysterious will. But the Community's capacity to see and appreciate the breadth of God was mind-expanding.

Anyone who maintained a doctrinaire position or a negative attitude to common life based on religious ideas would have seemed small minded. In this environment it was also easy to make the connections between the microcosm of community life and the larger issues of justice and mercy in society and in the world generally. If we gained so much from openness to others, ought not the same principle to apply on a larger stage?

"Seeing God in the other" is actually a principle that affirms the dignity of all human beings (not just community members!). It is a primary way in which God is known, and it is universal. It does not depend on acceptance of religious doctrines, but neither does it lose its truth because of objections to the idea of "God." When we are stripped to the core of our being, it does not matter whether we are a priest or a professor, a king or a cleaner. The characteristics of God that affirm our dignity coincide with all our deepest longings and aspirations. They are what we mean by salvation. They are what we pray for.

We might say that Paul's "body" image is as good a metaphor for humanity as it is for the church. "If one member suffers, all suffer with it." It is the suffering of the world that most clearly points to God. Where is the most pressing need for healing, liberation etc.? So it is in hearing and responding to one another as human beings, in understanding our connectedness to each other, that we begin to create an awareness of the God in whom we all live and move and have our being.

To affirm that "in him we live and move and have our being" has certain implications. We are not free-floating atoms in the universe. Our consciousness of our own and God's existence is part of a wider consciousness, from which we cannot detach ourselves. We may have passionate beliefs, but that does not mean our insights have a unique status, which trumps all other perceptions. Nor does it mean that other people's perceptions are "just as good" as mine. In the Community it was understood that it takes the whole body to know the mind of Christ—a principle that generally applies in a limited group as much as it does to the church universal.

Seeing things in this way does not always sit too well with the picture of God as a king in another world. In community, the natural milieu for God is the grubbiness of ordinary life rather than a celestial throne. Tolerance, affirmation, forgiveness, contentment with and acceptance of the provisional are characteristic of this experience of God—as opposed to the laws, certainties and judgments of some religious groups.

Of course, we do also need the sense of Otherness. It enables us to be profoundly stirred, moved, inspired and elevated. It gives us the sense of being called, invited, drawn almost in spite of ourselves to make a response. It speaks to the sense of being lost and in need of order, peace, security and meaning. But at the same time we also have a fundamental need for nearness. We need touch and contact. We find meaning in our humanity, with all its weaknesses and compromises. We are put in touch with a sense of the numinous, of mystery, by things that we can see and handle. We look for that which affirms our goodness rather than our badness, our connectedness rather than our separateness, our harmony with the universe rather than our dissonance. And when truth is understood as something to be discovered among us rather than merely handed down, God also needs a different shape.

A God who cannot survive except by being protected in a kind of religious cocoon will have only a limited following. Hence, for some, entering community was a bit of a shock to the religious system. Many of the ways in which they had been trained to talk about God seemed a bit gauche in this new setting. In a variety of ways, God was understood in a much more down to earth way than they were accustomed to. Yet that did not detract from a corporate worship that fed the sense of a transcendent God. On the contrary, it enhanced it, to a degree rarely experienced in ordinary church life.

It also seemed perfectly natural to think of God in a corporate rather than an individual way, or to think of God's action as, say, a touch, as opposed to thinking of a touch as a human *response* to God's prompting. God, in a word, was near, frequently encountered in the interplay of human relationships, and in this environment there was a distinct lack of dogma or legalism.

One question that might arise here is how does the consciousness of God described above fit in with the specifically Christian doctrine of the Trinity? The Trinity was certainly an important concept in community life because of its relational character. However, images such as Rublev's famous icon depicting three angelic figures are not necessarily the most helpful way to imagine God in the milieu of an "incarnate" Christian faith. They could reinforce the picture of God as an anthropomorphic being living in a separate world.

In reality the Trinity is a mystery, whose riches may be explored on different levels.

Most people who believe in God do not do so out of intellectual conviction but because God is an inescapable fact of their existence. It is often difficult to separate consciousness of God from the consciousness of one's own existence. Both seem a given, however we may discuss it philosophically. Hence the concept of the Trinity directly confronts the issue of identity, the notion that the "I" can be autonomous and self-sufficient. The fact that we only discover our identity as part of a wider corporate consciousness is not a mere sociological fact of life; it derives from the nature of being itself, which comes from the Creator and is fed by our worship.

The Trinity is a concept that expands the length and breadth of our understanding of God's presence in the world. Given that we tend to take on the characteristics of that which we worship, Trinitarian belief actually feeds an "incarnate" faith in ways that can be both unconscious and profound.

For many, then, community life was sacramental. Its meaning did not lie in its religious commitment, or even the recognition that Christian faith is more than just an individual thing. Its significance was ultimately in the way God was understood and encountered, whether or not every community member had a clear sense about that.

Chapter 21

Jesus

If "hearing God in the other" was mind expanding, it also brought up mixed feelings about Jesus. This stemmed from the ambiguities that attach to this person who is the most exalted religious figure in the world. In "renewal" movements Jesus is usually a divine figure of intense and enthusiastic devotion, the king of kings and lord of lords. In contrast, the earthly Jesus can seemingly be almost anything you want him to be, from a stern but kindly English gentleman to the champion of a liberation movement.

Obviously Jesus was a historical person. Christians are, theoretically, those who follow his teachings and beliefs. In practice, however, Christianity has been shaped less by the beliefs that Jesus held himself than by beliefs *about* him. "Christ," for example, is a belief about Jesus, and it is that word which has provided the name for the religion based on his life. Thus it is possible to bear the name "Christian" whilst not necessarily adhering to anything that the historical Jesus would have recognized as part of his teaching. "Christians" are those who believe that Jesus is the Christ; they are not always people especially known, for example, for loving their enemies or sitting light to possessions.

In theory there should be some correspondence between religious beliefs and the world of observation and experience, so that beliefs are seen to be reasonable because of what they lead to, as opposed to being arbitrary dogmas. However, sometimes the word "Jesus" seems detached from this correspondence. Jesus is "Lord," but the humanity that goes with that title varies considerably according to one's perspective. In these circumstances what is the content of the word "Jesus"? It seems that "Jesus" is effectively just another name for God, and as such may have no distinctive meaning.

For the Community this ambiguity led to a gradual divergence between the style of worship that fed its own life and the worship of the charismatic movement, which was often characterized by love songs to Jesus and adoration of him in his exalted state.

In the latter, the actual teaching of Jesus frequently seemed secondary to the proclamation of his divinity — as if that was the primary fact that needed to be asserted about him.

In the same way, the religious significance of his death as an atonement was often emphasized as if everything else he did was incidental. In effect, the role of historical truth was only to reinforce religious truth, which was the truth that mattered. Religious truth was contained in formularies, which, if believed, confirmed a person as one of the faithful, and if not believed, left him or her with nowhere to go. In community it was hard to imagine this as the situation that Jesus thought he was initiating.

Perhaps this sounds too harsh a judgment on the religious scene of the time. But it was more a matter of feeling than of explicit theology. There are many ways in which we give out messages, and this was one of the messages that seemed to come through the music and the language of "renewal." Community members felt the need to "be real," and a lot of contemporary charismatic worship felt unreal in various ways.

The historical Jesus was a unique individual who said and did things that were so radical and yet so liberating and so self evidently true that some called him the Son of God. They may not have meant all that is now meant by the Son of God, but that was the root of it. Hence in community there was a conviction that the title later conferred on Jesus cannot be separated from the real human life that gave rise to it.

Mainly Jesus' sayings commended themselves. Take the Sermon on the Mount. "Blessed are the meek." "Blessed are you poor." "Blessed are the peacemakers." These sayings cut across the norms of society even today. In that ancient, militaristic world, where human life was less than nothing, they were unheard of. Yet they commended themselves, not because of Jesus' divine status, but because we all instinctively know that human life would be infinitely better if it were like this. Jesus' sayings represent "salvation" for the human condition. In spiritual terms Jesus was a revelation of what it means to live a truly human life.

Thus a lot of community teaching focused on what Graham Pulkingham used to call "the simple sayings of Jesus." To *worship* Jesus was to take them on board, in personal lives and also in the way life and relationships were ordered.

In contrast, a one-sided focus on Jesus' divinity all but guaranteed his irrelevance, other than as a personal savior, guide and comforter of private, internal inadequacies. A good deal of popular worship of Jesus seemed more about establishing a connection with transcendence than with reproducing his life, possibly as a way of compensating for the perceived inadequacies of institutional religion.

Theologically speaking Jesus represents the "new Adam," a new kind of humanity. Community life brought this question quite sharply into focus. Put it this way: what is the difference between saying that God was in Christ and saying that God, by his Spirit, is in me? Did Jesus have an identity, a soul, which is not of this world? Was he a special agent from beyond the stars, assuming human form and here to carry out a religiously loaded task? Or was he a man, filled with the Spirit of God (as we too might potentially be) to such a degree that people called him the Son of God? Doctrine might well say that Jesus was fully divine and fully human, but in practice a lot depends on where the weight of our religious imagination lies.

It is less a matter of doctrine than of religious feeling: "hands that flung stars into space" (the "special agent" Jesus) or "I will hold the Christ-light for you" (the incarnate God)? Some might say there is room for both, but the reality is that religious consciousness is formed by the way we worship and the ideas contained in hymnody.

This can sometimes make integration difficult. A form of worship which is an expression of faith to one can seem far too other-worldly to another — and there is seemingly no way for the different perspectives to communicate. This was a common experience for community members.

By and large, the problem for the church, as the institutional guardian of religious belief, is that the religious significance of Jesus is inevitably seen as primary. It directs us to the contemplation of his person rather than to the realization of his sayings. It is dogmatic, stressing law rather than grace, personal "rightness with God" rather than justice. In belief and behavior it is essentially defensive of God and of God's supposed interests. But in real life, as Jesus lived it, law was often set aside or reinterpreted.

New truth emerged, in the form of spiritual wisdom or creative solutions to a problem. "Obedience to God" often meant going far *beyond* any requirement that the human mind might consider reasonable.

In ordinary church life the religious framework for many Christians tends to make a clear separation between the material world and the unseen, spiritual world in which God dwells. The cross and the resurrection stand at the interface between the two, so that the goal of religious activity is to get people to move, in their consciousness of belonging, from one sphere to the other, using Jesus and his sacrifice as the gateway. This makes Jesus an object of worship, but it's doubtful if Jesus himself saw it that way. *His* gospel is distinctly this-worldly.

If the focus is exclusively on Jesus' divinity, we either treat his sayings as laws or ignore them as an impossible ideal. However, his words are probably best understood as the expression of his Spirit. "Love your enemies" means, not "Thou shalt love thy enemies," but something more akin to "Why don't you love your enemies instead of hating them?" In other words, Jesus extended a radical vision to his hearers as wisdom to be taken up freely rather than a law to be obeyed, giving them room to breathe.

By asserting that Jesus is God, we are saying that this is how God relates to us too. Jesus *does* get angry and judgmental, but not at lawbreakers and various assorted sinners. His anger is directed at those who outlaw them in the name of God. *That* is what God is like, and that is where the authority of Jesus needs to be felt.

For example, take one of Jesus' famous sayings, on divorce. Why would you call a man who forbids divorce the Son of God? Or is it the other way round? Does Jesus' teaching on divorce have authority *because* he is the Son of God? It's likely most people today would say it was the second.

The teaching on divorce is tough, but we have to accept it because it was the Son of God who said it. But is that strictly true? The church made his teaching into a law, but in Matthew's version of the story it sounds as if Jesus is reacting to the emphasis on law in contemporary religious discourse. It's as if he is saying, "You want a law? I'll give you a law. Try this for size..."

He then gives a law that he knows is impossible to fulfill. Sure enough, his disciples respond that in that case it is better not to marry. But Jesus' point is that if we live by the law we fail. The law makes sinners of us all, *including Jesus himself.* That kind of deep wisdom is the reason why Jesus was called the Son of God.

The Gospels are full of examples of things Jesus said and did which essentially express the spirit of the man. For example, "You can't serve God and mammon (money)." In a modern industrial society that is very difficult to deal with. So, we say, we shouldn't be greedy. We shouldn't make an *idol* out of money. We should be *responsible* about the resources that God has entrusted to us.

We should give generously, but there's nothing wrong with money as such. (Notice all the "shoulds" and "shouldn'ts"?) Perhaps our inbuilt sense of guilt makes us look for a justification of our position. But Jesus was simply stating a fact of his life and experience, which was held out to us as a way of salvation, to be taken up freely.

Jesus also says, "Blessed is he who is not scandalized by me" (Luke 7.23). He is very much aware that the natural response to the gospel of the kingdom will be rejection—even righteous rejection. Some Christians assume the reason for this is opposition from satanic forces, or alternatively from the Jewish establishment whom Jesus criticized (we, of course, would never react as they did!).

Actually, it had more to do with the dynamics of human behavior, which affect all of us, religious or not. The tensions among human beings are always dealt with socially by a determination to separate the good from the bad, and to eliminate the bad. Religion often plays a crucial role in this process, as the arbiter of what "good" and "bad" are.

But God is totally outside this dynamic. He is not controlled by human responses and judgments. So what happens when God incarnate appears? He is not someone with magical powers but an ordinary man who in his spirit lives outside the normal human dynamic. Instead of condemning sinners he accepts and welcomes them. He says and does some outrageous things, yet with such wisdom and freedom of spirit that people listen to him gladly. Not all—especially not those who are the prime movers in the institutional dynamic. They are scandalized by Jesus' attitudes.

Jesus' attitudes are reflected throughout his sayings and in his ministry to various people from all kinds of backgrounds regardless of moral or political arguments, and in his defense of the "little ones" —in other words, those outside the structures of power. He adopted several approaches that undermined the basis of normal life. One involved various sayings such as "Have faith in God," "Don't be anxious," "Fear not." The thrust of these was that we do not secure our identity through acquisition, eliminating risk or guarding against what feels to us like death. Since all human life is, at root, based on this, Jesus' spirit confronts normal life at every level: money, standards of living, ambition, health, status, safety and security, social convention and so on.

Another tactic was in sayings such as "Love your enemies," or "Do good to those who hurt you," or in teaching such as Matthew 25: "as you did it to one of the least of these my brothers, you did it to me." Here he is talking about the ways in which we connect with others. Again, we have to take it that this is how God behaves, so this is how God-in-humanity behaves. Our relationship to the weak, the prisoners, the "little ones", is not governed by moral "oughts" but by identifying with the other. But if that is not where our heart is, then following Jesus presents a challenge.

A third approach, which Jesus was constantly using, was to stage dramas or cameos of the kingdom of God. Perhaps the word "stage" implies something contrived. Most of the things that Jesus did just happened, but they turned into stories.

A typical incident, for which Jesus took a lot of flak, was the story of Zacchaeus, the hated tax collector whose life was turned round because Jesus invited himself to supper. The biggest story or drama of them all, of course, was the cross — an extraordinary demonstration of the principles of the kingdom (for example, "fear not"). The medium of story is a powerful teaching tool (Jesus made up plenty of his own) because it bypasses abstract concepts and earths truth in everyday life. Thus the process of undermining the foundations of normal human life included stories, pithy sayings encapsulating spiritual truth, and demonstrations.

Community living proved that the human and divine Jesus must be understood and experienced as an indivisible reality. Too much focus on the divine, and we could get caught up in religious fervor and the excluding attitudes that seem to go with the defense of God. Lose sight of his divinity, and "God incarnate" turned into commonplace humanity, devoid of imaginative spiritual power to transform human life. The "simple sayings of Jesus" undermine even things considered immutable, such as the structures that govern social life. They do so, not by a different set of laws, but by imagination and the human spirit. There was also the recognition that for the most part Jesus' life cannot be lived, except in a weak and inadequate way, by individuals acting alone. Jesus' life is relational in terms of all the factors that hold human life together — money, sex, power, law, tradition, culture, shared beliefs and so on. Imagination and the spirit cannot transcend these things apart from human beings acting together.

Thus in the Community, the attempt to realize the "new Adam" was a corporate rather than an individual affair. Its characteristic phraseology— "a people of praise," "the simple sayings of Jesus," "the body of Christ"—reflected a desire to unite the human and the divine in a way that was true to the Spirit of Jesus. Here, as in the case of Jesus himself, God was to be found in the palpable (but also homely and ordinary) realities of human life. It would be wrong to suggest that the Community *modified* its worship of Jesus the divine Son of God—plenty of its songs indicate otherwise. But the sense of journey came about through the growing recognition that to truly worship Jesus is to explore his God-filled humanity in all its personal and corporate dimensions.

In truth "Jesus" needs to be worshiped and manifested in the life of the church. It is not that individuals cannot worship Jesus and reflect his life; obviously they can. But we do not see the real Jesus until we see the "new Adam" in all its dimensions.

That is a body of people, recognizing Jesus in each other, acting in concert to make the new humanity visible and drawing the spiritual resources for doing so from their worship. The reality often is that many factors militate against this in modern churches, and hence the pressure is to make the church service "relevant" or interesting — sometimes by a certain religiosity in the adulation of Jesus.

Chapter 22

Spirit

For Christians, the rediscovery of the Holy Spirit in the 1960s was exciting. At that time, the springtime of the movement, it was as if God was only a hairsbreadth away, liable to break into the sensory world of experience at any moment. No one knew what would happen next or where an activity of the Holy Spirit would lead to.

Living in community, sharing everything in common, was but one of many manifestations of God's presence, confirming the pattern attested to in the years immediately following Jesus' death and resurrection. That pattern was the kind of thing that came to be associated with the Holy Spirit: spontaneous and unpredictable, mysterious yet also dynamic, fresh and creative.

Today the word "spirit" is much more familiar, in religious or quasi-religious language, than it was 50 years ago. Within mainstream Christianity, the charismatic movement put the Holy Spirit on the map in a new way.

The Community of Celebration was very much a product of it. In the Community, people frequently talked about "following the Spirit" and its history includes a film made in 1970 by that name.

Ever since that time, both inside and outside the church, there has been a widespread increase in interest in "spirituality," a term that covers a range of activities or interests: meditation, worship, symbol or metaphor, music, experimental ideas and practices often lumped together under the generic heading of New Age.

The general sense of meaning engendered by "spirit" and "spirituality" is "incorporeal," "non-material," "relating to the mind or the soul."

In Christianity, "spirit" can sometimes mean something similar to "personality," an unseen presence, which may be benign or evil in its impact on humans. The Holy Spirit is often thought of in that way. "Spirit" often carries an implication that there are no boundaries. Anything goes. We can be under the control of "spirit," and when we are, we may behave in ways that are normally foreign to us. Perhaps this is why the word "spirit" was appropriated as a term for intoxicating liquor.

All this gives an impression that "spirit" refers to an unseen world inhabited only by the mind or the soul, and possibly by various unseen forces. In community, however, "spirit" was simply an ordinary, down to earth, human characteristic. If you were to describe a person as "filled with the Spirit," for example, the normal meaning would be someone whose ordinary demeanor or behavior is godly — not superhuman, as if intoxicated by some kind of alien substance. That did not rule out the possibility of empowerment from God.

The experience of empowerment, or "filling with the Holy Spirit," is part of the Christian tradition, but it does not change who we are or confer on us superhuman powers. "Charismatic" gifts, for instance, are natural human gifts. They all exist in human beings outside the church. Empowerment by the Holy Spirit may enable a gift to emerge and blossom, but in community life it was recognized that it would not turn someone into a leader, for example, who did not have that gift.

One weakness of the charismatic movement was that it concentrated attention on spiritual gifts, implying that these were supernatural manifestations unique to Christianity and were in fact the primary characteristic of the Holy Spirit's activity. Thus, a renewal whose most important aspect was the recovery of spiritual unity across huge divides in the church eventually became a movement focusing on certain specific features.

One of those features, generating both excitement and skepticism by degrees, was the miraculous. However, the word "miracle" originally did not imply a suspension of the laws of nature; it simply meant "a marvel."

The sense of wonder and astonishment has always been a fundamental aspect of the Christian experience, but it is a wonder at the experience of God ongoing in our lives. Christians need to grasp this; otherwise they fall into the trap of thinking that God chose to provide them with a parking slot whilst leaving innocent babies to starve to death in Ethiopia.

This is a spiritual way of relating, to see God in and thank God for everything. This is what it means to be filled with the Spirit.

It is true that in a certain kind of spiritual milieu some very remarkable things can happen. In Pentecostal and charismatic circles there are many such incidents, including reports of raisings from the dead — something that also occurred in the Community's origins in the sixties, at least in the sense that a woman certified dead by a doctor subsequently revived after prayer.

Although some may insist on scriptural principles in relation to such ministries, actually the foundation of them is not so much doctrine as *belief*: not dogmatic belief, but an environment where the presence of God acting by the Holy Spirit is taken for granted as part of the furniture of life. In such an environment it is expected that remarkable things will happen, and they do.

It may well be that there is a whole dimension of what it means to be spiritual beings which is lost or suppressed in modern rationalistic culture. But is charismatic experience of this type the limit of what we mean by "spirit," or even the norm, in

Christian faith? The tendency to make norms out of experience is a well known habit. It *can* be helpful up to a point. The Community used to study the scriptures, particularly the sayings of Jesus, and found many resonating with what it was doing and shedding light upon it. But it resisted building a theology of community from them.

A theology implies something fixed, applicable to others as well as to those reflecting on their particular experience.

In the same way the "Holy Spirit" experience of modern times has looked to the New Testament to shed some light on what is happening. It's a process as old as the New Testament itself: at Pentecost, Peter says, "This is what the prophet Joel was talking about." It's a way of grounding an experience, bringing it into the context of a spiritual tradition. It may *commend* it to others, but it does not *define* the way in which the Holy Spirit will always act or be experienced.

What community life seemed to highlight was that the life of Jesus was spiritual in a rather different sense from modern day charismatic or Pentecostal Christianity. He certainly ministered to individuals in various states of need—people who were sick or in some kind of bondage. But his emphasis was on what the life of God is like rather than on signs, which for him were simply the visible expression of a deeper reality.

Jesus also spent a good deal of time casting out demons. Whether such powers have any objective existence is a modern question; the fact is that their effect on individuals can be physically, psychologically and spiritually damaging. Clearly Christianity has something to say about this, if only because Christ is the one who sets captives free. It may well be that the language used is that of an outside agency, because of our felt need for help from a source outside all our projections and deceptions. Nevertheless that should not control our imagination to the point where God is merely a player in an unseen celestial struggle. The Jesus who sets the captives free is one and the same

Spirit who liberates individuals from their inner bondages and frees slaves or brings justice or gives people hope by fairer trade agreements. In community, spiritual life needed to reflect the same breadth.

Jesus also emphasized belief. But the belief was not that God will do miracles as such, but that God is alive and can be trusted; that he is untouched by the strategies we adopt to protect our lives.

We might express this in a cameo by saying that, in terms of Jesus' vision, there is no difference between a Christian who has life insurance and an atheist who has it. Neither believes in God in the way that Jesus did. Of course, in the end, the church had to accept that most people cannot fully live by the Spirit of Jesus. It made room for the monastic movement almost as a department of the church, which has the special function of preserving the memory of his vision.

In its early days the Community of Celebration was very much a charismatic community, "following the Spirit" as the saying goes, blurred at the edges as to its membership and fitting in well with the "renewal" scene at the time. Over a period, however, things were subtly changing. At one level there were issues to do with permanency, membership and the question of how to preserve the community's charism long term. In terms of spiritual life, there was the question of what was needed to nurture people involved in the closely-knit relational life of a community.

One of the attractions of the Community was the idea of living together in love, forging deep relationships, living as a family, maintaining a high level of commitment to one another, and so on. That is how it looked to the outsider, but anyone who has lived in a community knows that such a lifestyle can throw up significant problems. Community relationships are a bit like marriage; you cannot necessarily take the space you want, nor can you write the other person off and avoid them. There is a constant struggle with one's responses, which can often be in the form of projections from an earlier, forgotten time of unresolved pain. In order to grow (or even to survive) spiritually, these areas have to be examined and dealt with.

So a response to the Spirit that led to the radical step of community living also made it necessary to invite the same Spirit into the soul-depths, places where God was unknown because people did not even know they existed. There was talk of the inner journey and about finding God in the depths of one's being. It was a recognized problem in renewal, although issues of relationships and self-awareness generally were greatly intensified in the milieu of community life.

Community life required openness, not only to one's neighbor (closing the back door to withdrawal if relationships got sticky), but also to other people's perspectives. It meant drawing on a whole range of resources for dealing with these kinds of issues, which did not necessarily come from a charismatic or even a religious stable. It encouraged a kind of integration, in which the links that connected various aspects of human life—spiritual, psychological, social, political—were recognized. It affected many areas, including approaches to God and the Bible.

The language of "seeing God in one another" and "finding God in the depths" sound like an "immanent" God—a God who is "in" rather than "out there." But the sense of God as power from without was never abandoned in community life. For instance, at the same time that these internal issues were being explored the leaders at Post Green offered a slot when anyone who wished could come to receive prayer ministry.

One day, a woman came who had had to wear a neck brace for a long time. Later on the same day she mentioned that the tension in her neck was easing, and not long after removed the brace permanently. It was an example of how conventional ministry typical of charismatic groups sat alongside other approaches to spiritual life.

It was a similar story at the spring camps run by the community at Post Green. After evening worship, an opportunity was given for anyone to come forward for prayer. One night a woman came forward, and as soon as a hand was placed on her head she fell on the floor.

Later, it became a fad in certain circles, raising questions about its value and authenticity as a spontaneous happening. In this case, it seemed to be a genuine release, yet the teaching at the camps would hardly have generated that kind of response. In those days, the main focus of interest was on the inner journey and the political dimensions of the gospel.

What seemed to bring the two poles together was worship. Community worship was inclusive. It made room for all kinds of people and preferences and allowed them to be whatever they needed to be before God.

It was a vehicle through which anything could be offered to God — adoration or pain, joy or anger, faith or unbelief. It differed from many popular forms of worship in one crucial respect: it did not draw the worshiper totally away from earth into heaven. In contrast some popular forms of worship seemed escapist, making room for only a certain kind of spirituality or theological outlook.

The nature of Spirit, according to Jesus, is that it is like the wind: you don't know where it is coming from or where it is going. This is in direct contrast to law, which provides a firm basis for action and predictable consequences for non-compliance.

Law is a way of keeping control; Spirit, by its very nature, is creative. It comes up with an original idea and takes it somewhere, which is very unsettling for those who like to know where they are, so that they can control the situation and especially know their own place in it. The Spirit does not divide and separate, like law; it does not judge; it does not control. The Spirit is near, flexible, non-rational (not irrational), ready to come up with a creative solution. It is also vulnerable; it can be squelched or hurt. All these characteristics were reflected in one way or another in community life.

The Spirit is also known in the New Testament as the Paraclete. This is a forensic term, which means the defense counsel. The defense is the opposite number to the prosecution, who is the accuser. In other words, it is part of the Spirit's function to counter accusation, from whatever source. A big preoccupation of the New Testament has to do with dealing with the voice of the accuser.

How does the Paraclete "defend" us? The Spirit is the Spirit of Jesus, which for practical purposes means a spirit that inspires us to live like he did. To the extent that we have that Spirit, we are free from the power of accusation, because God does not accuse. We may be wrongly accused, either by others or by our own internal voices that condemn us, but Jesus' Spirit protects us from the power of accusation to control and cripple our lives.

The supreme example of this was Jesus' voluntary death on the cross, demonstrating a spirit that cannot be controlled or suppressed by the powers that govern human life and relationships, even in the face of the most extreme circumstances and even in the face of accusation by those who are the representatives of God.

To the extent that we have that Spirit, we cannot be touched by accusation. The accusation is the accusation of *those who keep the law*, who might be others or simply our own bad conscience. The law might be right, but our law breaking is not the problem so far as God is concerned.

The problem is the refusal, on the part of our accusers, to believe that God who is totally other than us does not participate in our systems of law and guilt.

Community life tried to give people a small taste of this: an irrepressible spirit in the face of secular and religious convention, and freedom from accusation which was a big cause of personal problems. A spirit of celebration was enshrined in its name and in the title of recordings such as *Celebrate the Whole of it.*

On the one hand, life was lived in a certain way, celebrating the sayings of Jesus, as it were, by living with very little money, sharing resources, committing lives to one another. On the other hand, individual members were very frail human beings. There was plenty of pain, anger, hurt, frustration and what the church would like to call sin. But everyone was accepted "in the beloved," to use a term from Ephesians 1.6, regardless of their condition, and all of it was brought before God in worship. The spirit of the Community had a liberating effect on many who had been hurt or were condemned by their own frailty.

A problem for some was the attitude of families towards those who joined community. There could be a feeling that you were abandoning one family in favor of another. In some cases there were issues about money or inheritance. There was nothing in this kind of reaction that could be called "Christian," yet it commonly came from religious people. There was really no defense in terms of argument, and it could be a source of guilt feelings. But the spirit of the life was its own justification for those who lived it, and it often disarmed the fears.

One of the primary characteristics of the Spirit of Jesus is imagination. It takes a lot of imagination to look at the way life is lived now and to visualize something different as a real practical possibility. To do so will mean going against entrenched and accepted beliefs and will also involve, in all probability, a considerable loss or sacrifice on the part of some people. The loss could be a material loss or a loss of valued convenience, status or relationships. It could even be the loss of cherished notions and beliefs. To an extent this was the experience of those who began to "think outside the box," to use current jargon, in the beginnings of Celebration history.

But the benefit of living by the spirit of Jesus is joy; indeed, he says as much when he tells his disciples, "I have meat to eat that you know nothing about" (John 4.32). We tend to think of joy as an internal feeling of gladness, and indeed it can be. But it can also be very difficult for an individual to experience joy. It may be experienced only fleetingly, as when a person has had some good fortune. Often, its absence is accounted for by depression, discontentment, boredom or general frustration with life. These are not easily shaken off, and may be compounded by a feeling of failure stemming from our belief that, as Christians, we *ought* to be feeling joyful. Hence the Community tried to express the joy of Jesus in a corporate way, by a spirit of celebration.

Celebration seemed to create the space for the happy and the sad to be glad together. It did not require a particular *feeling*. Yet it undoubtedly captured something of the spirit of what Jesus was talking about. What might, in other circumstances, have been experienced as a sacrifice or a deprivation was accepted cheerfully as their way of life. People were fed by it. Jesus urged his disciples to count the cost of following him, but to those who did it never seemed like a cost.

In summary, there is a widespread constituency in the church for whom "the Spirit" is not of this world, or if it is, it belongs to an interior world of the soul. "The Spirit" is thought of as a manifestation of God who operates in certain characteristic if mysterious ways. But this can limit the way God is known, and it limits the possibilities. It can also be divisive, because there is often an aura of righteousness, or correctness, which implies that things must be experienced, or believed, or interpreted in a certain way. But there is another way in which God is known, and that is by the spirit of the man Jesus.

It is the spirit which rescued Zacchaeus, absolved the woman taken in adultery, healed people on the Sabbath, which told people to go the second mile, love their enemies, not to be anxious about their lives or to give thought to standards of living (food and clothes), to serve him by serving the "little ones."

As Christians have thought about those things, the implications have been understood in a wide range of social and political ways.

Unless these two ways of encountering God come together, one may become irrelevant to all but those who are interested in that kind of thing, while the other may pursue activities that could just as well be done (and often are) by secular agencies. Here, the scope of Jesus' *imagination* is lost. It is an imagination that constantly comes up with creative solutions, and imagines them into reality with joy and celebration.

It isn't easy to hold the two perspectives together without sliding off in one direction or the other. The pressures are felt within the church, in theology and a number of social issues.

For many people in the Community of Celebration, life in community seemed to involve something of a journey from one perspective to the other. But it was worth the effort, for in the end what the church has to offer to the world is not a religious message, or even sacrificial works, but the Spirit that comes from God.

IV EPILOGUE

Chapter 23

Community and the Church

L ooking back from a 21st century perspective, what impact if any did the Community of Celebration have on the life of the church? Any assessment would have to include not only the Community but also the roots out of which it came, the extraordinary period of parish renewal that occurred at the Church of the Redeemer in the 1960s.

For many people, the primary impact was in terms of music in worship. The Fisherfolk were a worldwide phenomenon and they were the Community's most high profile ministry. As far as popular church culture is concerned, it looks as though the excellence of 30-40 years ago has now dwindled to a vestige. People have moved on and the world of music in worship has changed enormously. But popular culture is not necessarily the best guide to determine what is lasting or ultimately significant.

What the Community promoted over 3 or 4 decades was a kind of blended music, mainly in the Anglican Church. It had to do both with the way songs were arranged and sung and with a repertoire that combined the contemporary and the traditional. There is plenty of documentary evidence that the repertoire continues in use, inasmuch as royalty income remains constant to the present day—most of it from churches in the USA and UK, and also in Australia. Songs are included in weekly bulletins or overhead projections, and declared in their annual CCLI copyright license.

That is one way to look at it. Whenever there is a movement of the Spirit, in worship or anything else, for a while it seems that everyone is doing it. Then it stops. The question is how much of the former style will remain as part of the church's repertoire? One aspect of that is what makes it into the official church hymnals. Normally only a tiny fraction of what is produced achieves that kind of longevity.

One example among the Community of Celebration copyrights is Kathleen Thomerson's *I Want to Walk as a Child of the Light*, which has been translated into many languages including Chinese, Japanese and Korean. Another is Edith McNeil's little song *The Steadfast Love of the Lord*, which is one of the most popular songs on the CCLI list, as is Max Dyer's *I will sing, I will sing*. These songs are not only used by Anglican Churches; they find their way into other denominational songbooks and hymnals as well.

The worship scene today, particularly in ECUSA which has more of a choral tradition than the English church, is extremely polarized. On the one hand there are those who are trying to revive the tradition of the Royal School of Church Music in Anglican worship. At the other extreme is contemporary worship, media driven with people performing on a stage, a wall of sound coming from the front which carries on regardless of whether the congregation participates or not. In between are those who have probably been the most influenced by, and identified with, the worship of the Community of Celebration.

These are people who mainly just do whatever they feel best in their own church — they hardly impact the great scene which is where the polarity lies.

There is a point of view that would say the only thing that matters in worship is what I like and what works for me. Many of those would see the worship of the Fisherfolk as belonging to the era of Joan Baez and Bob Dylan. It is passé, along with the beliefs and the worldview that inspired it. But there are also others, perhaps with longer roots, who recognize the impact that the Community had. It is not that there is a desire to turn the clock back, but there is an appreciation of something enduring. People sometimes visit or connect through the internet with comments such as "At last I've found you after 25 years. I've never found anything as satisfying as your blend of music." It is surprising how affected some can be even today through participation in what is essentially simple worship in the Community, even if their own tastes in music are very different.

What some may do is turn Fisherfolk songs into a rock idiom, where the strum, the drive and the tempo fit that genre. But behind all this is a cyclical phenomenon. Some of those who bought into modern profit and media driven worship are now finding it unsatisfying in the long run. It fails to nourish spiritual life over the long haul, so what they do is go back to the old nineteenth century hymns and put them into a rock idiom.

Yet Charles Wesley wrote over 6000 hymns of which only around 20 or so made it into the Episcopal Church Hymnal. So it is with Fisherfolk songs. Most of the corpus is material now used only by the Community of Celebration and similar groups. But in the USA at least, people will take material from a period when theology was more involved with the text, with a tune that was originally a folk melody from England, and dress it up in the clothes of what makes sense in the contemporary scene. This is one way in which some are now trying to find a more substantial corporate worship.

In terms of theology and lifestyle, there has been a similar process of assimilation and cyclical rediscovery. In the late 1960s people began to discover the concept of community and its importance for Christian discipleship. Soon there was a strong, widespread urge to change lifestyle and experiment with new ways of living, bringing church and secular life together in a variety of para-church forms. Then, in the 1980s, it was as if the tap was turned off. People moved on, often in an aggressive pursuit of material success. Later still there was a new kind of movement, particularly amongst young Christians involved in difficult urban situations, to join together again in some form of sharing. It looks different from the experiments of the 1960s and 1970s, but the basic impulse is quite similar. In Britain, the impulse often surfaces under the name of movements such as "Fresh Expressions," "emerging church" or "new monasticism."

The word "movement" may be too definitive to describe these developments. It implies there is a form of articulated theology, theory or practice.

In reality it is more a matter of outlook, people discovering kindred spirits or approaching problems in similar ways. It comes more from the grassroots than from the hierarchy, and there are many aspects to it that are similar to what was happening in the origins of the Community of Celebration.

For example, much of the present impetus comes from roots in charismatic theology, just as it did in the early community days. There is a willingness now, as then, to look at the strengths and weaknesses of church traditions, and to try to recover what has been lost. Thus in the Community's origins there was a strong critique of clericalism and its effects (though not throwing the baby out with the bath water) and rediscovery of the genius of the Book of Common Prayer for the spiritual life of the laity. Today, there are similar challenges and questions about the role of ordination. There is also renewed interest in the concept of a rule of prayer for ordinary Christians.

In the Community's origins the most powerful metaphor of spiritual life was the body of Christ, with its Pauline imagery of all the members belonging to one another in a single organ. In this context the five-fold ministry of Christ outlined in Ephesians 4 (apostles, prophets, evangelists, pastors and teachers) held a special significance. No one individual had all the gifts necessary to fulfill the needs of the body. Gifts were widely distributed and needed to have a proper outlet. In practice, however, the last two in the Ephesians 4 list (pastors and teachers) have tended to be hived off as the special preserve of ordained clergy. This is still an issue in today's grassroots movements.

Of course, there are churches, and forms of churchmanship, where ordination is less of an issue because of theology or ecclesiology. But those churches have their own issues. It is not a matter of saying that this is better than that, but of drawing on what is good in other traditions in order to supplement one's own. In early days at the Church of the Redeemer, for example, the pioneers received a lot of teaching and encouragement from the pastor of a Pentecostal church. This is a process that works both ways, and so it is today. People involved in experimental forms of church are often willing to look at traditions other than their own in order to create new forms for today's conditions.

Within the Community the concept of the priesthood of all believers was worked out in practice within an Anglican setting. It was not a dogma, defining churchmanship. It was taken for granted that the fundamental authority to minister was baptism, not ordination. This made it possible to experiment with lay presidency at the Eucharist, though it was always combined with celebration by an ordained minister—not only out of deference to church authority but also to reinforce the notion that the ministry of Christ is something shared. Later, the Community felt no need to continue the practice, but the fact that it was possible was important. It has an obvious resonance with situations where people are working on the margins of the church or where ordained ministry is not available.

The central issue is the empowerment of the laity.

Some denominational churches may feel they do that, but it is not really a question about church order. Empowerment of the laity at the Church of the Redeemer happened in the context of the historic liturgy and the episcopate, and was all the more powerful because of it. The problem with models is that they all too quickly turn into blueprints, or even worse, dogmas, whereas a movement of the Spirit is more about sensibility, a recognition, say, that leadership needs to be more collegial in character, or that leadership is more about enabling and facilitating than about controlling and directing.

In some ways the Community of Celebration was a product of its time; in others, ahead of its time. It came into being in a time of social change in which not only the church but various groups in secular society such as the hippie movement were experimenting with communes and other new ways of living. But for some at the heart of it, it was more than an experiment; it was their way of following the Spirit in a lifelong process. Where that led ultimately was to a ministry of presence in an urban ghetto.

In the course of that journey a great many issues were addressed: the division of sacred and secular, the control of church life by secular norms, the importance of being human in religious life, commitment and openness in Christian discipleship, the priority of love, willingness to examine the inherent weaknesses of one's own beliefs, issues of authority and leadership, the gospel imperatives of justice and mercy, the centrality of prayer and worship as the foundation of spiritual life. In particular there has been an insight into the nature of church as an organic body in which all belong to one another—a notion that is not the mark of a closed club, but a spiritual grace that the church has to offer to a divided society. It is a grace that links former members of the Community of Celebration around the world to the present day.

In one way or another, modern movements are seeking to address similar issues, whether at the local level of trying to connect with people who no longer feel the need for church as it has been known in the past, or on the wider stage, addressing religious factionalism and the great issues of justice and peace. Perhaps the basic question is simply what does it mean to be a Christian today? The answer, in whatever form it takes, will lie in the real commitment of ordinary human lives, not in conformity to religious ideology.

For the Community of Celebration, the commitment of human lives in worship led first to an extraordinary phenomenon in which huge resources were released for ministry, gifts of the laity were released and worship itself was transformed to the point that it became a worldwide fashion in the church. Later, in the way that such things come and go, the great scene moved on and commitment of lives had a different dimension.

No longer was it a matter of numbers and resources and dramatic but essentially short term effects. It now became a commitment of much fewer lives over the long haul, and this had quite a different kind of effect, the effect of a stable praying presence in a situation of need.

It is impossible to analyze the effects of prayer, but Christians believe in it because they can often feel its effects before they see tangible results. Subtle changes take place in the spiritual climate, or straws in the wind herald new developments that eventually become a critical mass for larger change. Such a process often takes many years, but it is just as much a part of "following the Spirit" as the breathtaking roller coaster ride of youthful days when people were willing to move home and even country at the drop of a hat. The Community today is beginning to see some of the results of its years of commitment to Aliquippa, in the shape of the gifts and resources of other agencies coming to the town and finding a hospitable base, both spiritual and material, in the Community and its facilities.

As Jesus said, following the Spirit is like going with the wind: you never know where it will take you. For those involved with the Community of Celebration, it has taken them half way round the world and back, in the process shedding dozens of participants who are now scattered throughout the English speaking world. It has led both to a dynamic life of constant change and to the patience of a long haul, to large numbers and small. In its present life, ministry gifts are being added by others with a similar concern for the town. Like the Apostle Paul's comment about the variety of gifts, this too comes from the same Spirit.

For further information about the Community, write to Celebration, PO Box 309, 809 Franklin Avenue, Aliquippa PA 15001, USA.
Email: mail@communityofcelebration.com
Website: www.communityofcelebration.com

BOOKS

O is a symbol of the world, of oneness and unity. In different cultures it also means the "eye," symbolizing knowledge and insight. We aim to publish books that are accessible, constructive and that challenge accepted opinion, both that of academia and the "moral majority."

Our books are available in all good English language bookstores worldwide. If you don't see the book on the shelves ask the bookstore to order it for you, quoting the ISBN number and title. Alternatively you can order online (all major online retail sites carry our titles) or contact the distributor in the relevant country, listed on the copyright page.

See our website www.o-books.net for a full list of over 500 titles, growing by 100 a year.

And tune in to myspiritradio.com for our book review radio show, hosted by June-Elleni Laine, where you can listen to the authors discussing their books.

MySpiritRadio